SPIRITUAL INTELLIGENCE
Knowing God and Making Him Known

KIRBY AND SANDRA CLEMENTS

CLEMENTS FAMILY
MINISTRIES

DECATUR, GA

Address inquiries to the publisher:

Clements Family Ministry
2000 Cathedral Place
Decatur, Georgia 30034 USA

Learn more about the authors and their ministry at:
www.clementsfamilyministry.com

ISBN: 978-0-9794181-2-9
LCCN: 2012943014

First Printing: June 2012

Printed in the United States of America

Edited and composed by Annette R. Johnson, Allwrite Publishing

DEDICATION

We were looking for something that was eternal, dependable and good. We desired to invest our lives in a quest pleasing to God. We were searching for something to emulate and to pursue that was worthy of passing on to our family. We were looking to commit ourselves and our family to something, where at the end of the earthly sphere, there would be no regrets nor doubts. Our search ended in Him, Christ Jesus the Lord. And now our desire is to know Him and the power of His resurrection and be made conformable to His likeness.

ACKNOWLEDGEMENTS

We would like to thank Annyce Stone and Annette Johnson for their assistance with this work.

INTRODUCTION

The New Testament epistles seem to indicate that the battleground of our faith has always been conceptual, the struggle in interpreting historic truths, facts, and events and putting them into some practical, manageable form. The issue has either been the inability or the unwillingness to properly interpret and integrate redemptive truths and facts into life experiences. This may account for the apostolic exhortations to add knowledge to faith. It may be the reason behind the apostolic prayer for the disciples to be filled with a dimension of the Holy Spirit beyond the original baptism. This conceptual crisis may account for the falling away of the Galatians; the sustained immaturity of the Hebrews; the lawlessness of the Corinthians; and the mixture among the Colossians. It becomes obvious that the apostolic exhortations to "grow in grace and in the knowledge of the Lord," and to be "steadfast and immovable" are invitations to a sphere of intelligence that promote productive stewardship in the Kingdom of God. The appearance of these historic challenges in our contemporary redeemed community suggests a similar deficiency. While there is no deficit of faith or a lack of religious intelligence, there may be a need for spiritual understanding. In essence, there may be a need for an intelligence that comprehends the Divine-human connection with all of its privileges, promises, and responsibilities.

This work is based upon this premise. It is a collection of writings comprising more than three decades of experiences both within and beyond the church walls. Having served as a pastor and later a bishop in a megachurch with a variety of racial, cultural, ethnic, and generational groups, my experiences include every aspect of church life. My role as a bishop continues to allow me to be involved in all variations of churches based upon age, congregation size, racial and ethnic compositions, types of leadership, physical facilities, outreach capabilities, doctrinal and theological expressions. While involved in these liturgical and clerical responsibilities, my wife and I maintain a dental practice with a specialty in Prosthodontics. These topics, although not exhaustive, represent wisdom and knowledge gained from the Scripture, Holy Spirit and personal experiences in both the natural and spiritual world.

These writings are catalogued under the title of "Spiritual Intelligence," a phrase coined to express the idea that knowledge, wisdom, understanding, and discernment are not limited to academics. These topics are interconnected and represent dimensions of understanding that contribute to the idea of spiritual intelligence. The papers present the idea of salvation as a comprehensive process that is spiritual, psychological, and behavioral. The promises, privileges, and responsibilities of this process are mediated through the Holy Spirit and the Scriptures. While the Holy Spirit is received as power, the intelligence of God is to be found in the Scriptures. These papers reveal the significance of sound concepts and the quality of faith in the life of the believer. This is especially true regarding issues such as the nature and character of God; the supernatural and psychic phenomena; the quality of faith; and sociological factors such as gender, aging, spiritual, mental and physical well-being.

Our hope is that this work will develop a sensitivity, awareness and consciousness of the existence of the Divine and the spiritual, and their integration into the human and natural. As believers, we are called to influence the world in which we live. We accomplish this through conviction, credibility, and competence. We must be able to maintain a redemptive consciousness while living in a world of many ideas, knowledge, values, and objectives. While the world is not so interested in everything we do in the worship experience, it cannot neglect the power dynamic of the Holy Spirit, our insight, foresight, compassion, and awareness of things seen and unseen. We can comprehend and integrate spiritual truths into the natural sphere of the home, marketplace, and even the church. The ultimate expectation is that this work will help us all to know Him more and make Him known.

CONTENTS

II. MAKING HIM KNOWN

1

WHAT EXACTLY IS SPIRITUAL INTELLIGENCE?

Intelligence is an umbrella term describing the capacity for learning, reasoning, understanding, and similar forms of mental activity. It is the aptitude to grasp truths, relationships, facts, meanings, and to learn from past experiences, to plan, and solve problems. In fact, there is the recognition of multiple intelligences that describe the ability to understand space, time, language, math, logic, music, nature, and people.

There is also an intelligence that describes the aptitude of perceptions, intuitions, and even phenomena beyond sensory data. This is the capacity to understand truths, facts, meanings, relationships, functions, and realities that are seen, unseen, heard and not heard. There is the degree of sensitivity or awareness. It is a consciousness that is a product of a redemptive process.

IQ is the acronym for intelligence quotient, and refers to a score given for standardized intelligence tests. But not all intelligence can be measured by an IQ test. In fact, IQ measures mathematical, spatial, reasoning, logical ability, language understanding, but it is an inadequate measurement of the ability to comprehend data that is beyond the natural and sensory realm. There is an intelligence behind faith, courage and obedience. Otherwise, it is presumption. There is an ignorance behind rebellion and sin. When Divine revelation and interpretation is a scarcity, human ignorance is at a premium.

Knowing God

"SI" is the acronym for spiritual intelligence and is a measure of experiential and practical abilities. It is a quantification of sensitivity, awareness or consciousness of the existence and integration of the Divine and human, or rather the spiritual and the natural. It expresses the capacity to comprehend purposes, meanings, and the relationship between faith, belief, convictions, attitude, and behavior. It encompasses the identity of self and life's true values. It recognizes times and cycles. Ultimately, it corresponds to the degree of conformity to the likeness of Christ Jesus. The apostolic epistles are intended to raise the consciousness of the believers in the knowledge of the finished work of Christ. This is especially true of the letters to the Corinthians in which Paul seeks to replace carnality with spirituality (1 Cor. 3:1-22). Paul does not desire that their confidence and assurance be dependent upon the values, wisdom, and knowledge of this present world (1 Cor. 2:5). In fact, the Ephesian epistle contains the prayer that believers be filled with the spirit of wisdom and understanding in the knowledge of Christ (Eph. 1:15-23). However, the carnality of the Corinthian church is a reflection of spiritual ignorance.

SI is Christian, but it is not religious. Whereas the latter may measure an understanding of doctrines, dogmas, and disciplines, and core beliefs, SI is the ability to know God and make Him known. It is the genius of understanding Divine presence and purpose; Divine involvement in human affairs; and the strategies necessary for human response. It removes the boundary between the sacred and the secular in recognizing the interrelationship between the spiritual, natural, heavenly, and earthly. It recognizes the dimensions of Divine liability and human responsibility. It is developed sensitivity which is an awareness of the delicate balance between listening and speaking and hearing the sound of words but also listening for their meaning. All of these principles are apparent in the Pharisees, who were religious but lacked a true understanding of God (Matt. 9:12-13; 12:1-8). Their religion and concepts of God separated them from the very people who needed them (Luke 7:36-50). While the Pharisees demonstrated a zeal of God, their attitude toward those outside of their religious boundaries was void of compassion and understanding. They failed to understand that the heart of the Law was mercy and not sacrifice (Matt. 9:13).

Whereas a high IQ score records mental capacities and academic comprehension, such intelligence can be void of compassion, benevolence, and a common concern for anything or anyone beyond self. In fact, it can display itself in arrogance, pride, injustice, impatience, deceit, and a disdain for anything outside the sphere of what it values. It can be present without a knowledge or reverence for anything that is Divine or eternal. Such intelligence can boast itself of all forms of unrighteous conduct. It can even devise strategies for mass destruction. In our contemporary society, the 911 tragedy of the World Trade Center and the Oklahoma City bombing are classic examples of spiritual ignorance in the presence of zeal, conviction, and technical abilities. The bombers clearly had some form of academic intelligence but no reverence for life.

Making Him Known

Spiritual intelligence in itself is inseparable from integrity, humility, compassion, benevolence, awareness, sensitivity, courage, adaptability, spontaneity, and otherliness. In fact, it must display itself in justice, godliness, brotherly kindness, charity, and temperance. It is a knowledge and reverence for that which is Divine and eternal. Consequently, there is evidence of its presence in the operational behavior that is normal for a human being. A deficiency of these characteristic is found in the example of Rehoboam, who forsook the counsel of the elders and gave heed to the advice of his peers (1 Kings 12:6-20). His insensitivity and pride were reflection of spiritual ignorance. Paul exhorts the Ephesian elders to take note of themselves and the flock over which the Lord has made them overseers (Acts 20:28). In essence, the apostle exhorts the elders to do justice, love mercy and walk humbly before the Lord. True spiritual intelligence, as Paul encourages, is obedience to God.

Spiritual intelligence is not mysticism, sensationalism, nor irrationality. Each of these traits is the evidence of the separation of the Word from the Spirit. To the contrary, spiritual intelligence encapsulates the academic and integrates all spheres of intelligence, including common sense. Misconception of these principles is the example of the seven sons of Sceva who sought to exercise spiritual ministry without a fundamental understanding of the Word and Spirit (Acts 19:14-17). They sought to emulate Paul without the power of the Spirit. Likewise, the Samaritans were deceived by sorcery because of their ignorance of these principles (Acts 9:5-15).

While intelligence is expressed in academic and even religious issues, there can be an ignorance of the person, purposes, and ways of God. God made known His acts to Israel, but He only revealed His ways to Moses (Psalm 103:7). Paul experiences such spiritual ignorance among the Athenians who worship the "unknown God" (Acts 17:16-34). A spiritual deficit is also expressed in the encounter of Acquila and Priscilla with Apollos who was mighty in the Scripture but deficient in the more critical aspects of the faith (Acts 18:24-28). The ultimate expression of spiritual intelligence is the emulation of Christ Jesus in His relationship with the Father and His ministry to people.

Finally, spiritual intelligence is expressed in the manner in which we manage our own humanity. Paul encourages Timothy to be an example of the believer (1 Tim. 4:12). As aforementioned, Paul exhorts the Ephesian elders to exercise discipline and integrity as they minister to the people (Acts 20:28). They are to serve as examples to the people of God. The apostle reminds Timothy that men shall display their spiritual ignorance when they depart from the faith and exhibit all types of inordinate behavior (1 Tim. 4:1-3; 2 Tim. 3:1-5). When Israel ceased to glorify God and lost consciousness of the true and living God, their spiritual ignorance contributed to all kinds of unethical and immoral behavior (Rom. 1:21-32).

Even in our contemporary faith communities, there are expressions of spiritual ignorance. The display of rebellion, selfishness, sexual perversions, greed, avarice, oppression, exploitation and all forms of unrighteousness conduct are all forms of spiritual ignorance. This can also be seen in the display of gifts and callings without sanctification or charisma without character. Indeed, there is the existence of free will, but spiritual intelligence awakens the heart and mind to the attitude and behavior necessary to walk in righteousness.

Spiritual intelligence is a powerful ally to righteous living, but spiritual ignorance is expressed in racial, gender, and socioeconomic prejudices. Our convictions and beliefs regarding human relationships should not be dictated by the cultural norms but by Scripture.

Summary

*Intelligence describes a person's aptitude or intellectual ability.
*IQ is the acronym for intelligence quotient, referring to a score given for standardized intelligence tests.
*Academic intelligence is beneficial in the natural realm and can

result in arrogance, pride, injustice, impatience, deceit, and a lack of knowledge or reverence for anything that is Divine.

*Religious intelligence, or knowing *about* God, measures an understanding of doctrines, dogmas, and disciplines, and core beliefs. It can result in self-righteousness without the expression of love.

*Spiritual intelligence describes the aptitude of perceptions, intuitions, and even phenomena beyond sensory data. It is the capacity to understand truths, facts, meanings, relationships, functions, and realities that are seen, unseen, heard and not heard.

*SI is the acronym for spiritual intelligence.

*In knowing God, spiritual intelligence is a comprehension of the salvation experience and its privileges, promises, and responsibilities. It expresses the capacity to comprehend purposes, meanings, and the relationship between faith, belief, convictions, attitude, and behavior.

*In making God known, spiritual intelligence is the degree of conformity to the likeness of Christ Jesus.

I
KNOWING GOD

1
KNOWING GOD

2

SENSITIVITY

There is an intelligence that is cultivated when the dimensions of our world are enlarged. When we allow new ideas, beliefs, and even people into our sphere of consciousness, then knowledge and understanding increases. This acquired consciousness is a cultivated sensitivity, or "otherliness," through which we transcend selfishness, observe others and respond. Without it, love is simply an emotion; faith is simply stubbornness and personal ambition; and hope is empty optimism. Thus, sensitivity functions as guidance to faith, character to hope, compassion to knowledge, and patience to love.

As a component of spiritual intelligence, sensitivity is a developed awareness of our environment and all of its inhabitants. It is the delicate balance between speaking and being quiet. It is hearing the sound of words while listening for their meaning. It is the subjection of human emotions and desires to principles, so it cannot be confused with emotionalism.

Through His example, the Lord Jesus gives us the opportunity to develop sensitivity. His personal encounters with the sick, infirmed, confused, desperate, arrogant, proud, educated, ignorant, rich, poor, and all dimensions of humanity presented the opportunity for us to witness the origin and development of true, genuine sensitivity. He was keenly aware and responsive to the weaknesses and struggles of humanity. Using the parable of the Good Samaritan, He demonstrated the contrast between awakened compassion and an insensitivity generated by religious bias and over commitment to lesser things (Luke 10:30-37). He was spiritually conscious of the touch of one desperate woman while surrounded by a massive crowd of people (Matt. 9:20-22; Mark 6:25-34; Luke 8:43-45). During the agony of the cross, He was aware of His mother's anguish (John 19:27). All of these accounts express a virtue that is indispensable for Christian life and ministry.

Summary

*Sensitivity is a developed awareness of our surroundings and the ability to respond appropriately in love.

*Sensitivity is a cultivated "otherliness."

*Sensitivity involves the emotions, but also principles.

*The potential to become naturally sensitive is inherent but spiritually sensitive is not.

3

SPIRIT-BAPTIZED MINDS

The presence of the Holy Spirit in our lives is no substitute for sound beliefs and sound minds. We receive the Holy Spirit as power and not as intelligence (Luke 24:29; Acts 1:8). The intelligence of God is found in the Scripture (Matt. 22:29). While the Holy Spirit enables our minds to comprehend the core message of the Scripture, it does not inform our minds intellectually. For this reason, the battleground of our faith has usually been conceptual. Thus, denominational differences have been a matter of the interpretation of the Word.

When, for instance, the Bible says God is love (1 John 4:8-10), everyone believes and understands that God is loving and kind. However, believers disagree on the full expression of that love. Some assert, based on this, that God doesn't judge sin, and others believe that His love means they will have a trouble-free life. The former ignores the fact that God is holy while the latter overlooks the reality of a fallen world.

While the Scriptures are inspired and trustworthy as the source of doctrine, there has always been possibility of a misinterpretation of their true meaning (2 Tim. 3:15-17). Peter mentions certain individuals who misinterpret the writings and messages of Paul (2 Peter 3:15-16). The apostle encourages the disciples to add knowledge to their faith, suggesting that there can be a reliance upon the Lord without a proper understanding (2 Peter 1:5-9). Paul warns Timothy to be aware of false teachers and the influence of erroneous information (1 Tim. 1:19-20; 4:1-3; 2 Tim. 2:15-18; 3:14-17; 4:3-4). For this reason, the character of our faith is dependent upon the integrity and quality of the gospel that we have heard and believed. There can be spiritual illiteracy in the presence of zeal and enthusiasm. In essence, the mind needs to be baptized with truth.

Ephesians 1 is an avalanche of 206 words in a single sentence. This is perhaps one of the longest sentences in literature, and it extols the magnificence of God. In this text, Paul writes by revelation the prayer for the Ephesians that they may be filled with the Spirit of wisdom and revelation in the knowledge of Christ (Eph. 1:13-23). The apostle is aware of the need for spiritual literacy among the Ephesians. Even though they have been sealed by the Holy Spirit, their minds needed illumination.

The presence of faith is not synonymous with understanding. While there may be a reverence for God and the truths of the faith, there can be significant deficit of other characteristics. Indeed, faith comes by hearing the Word of God, but there can be a deficiency of information and misinterpretation of historical facts (2 Cor. 11:3-4). As believers, we have the privilege to hear all information, but we do not have the luxury to believe everything that we hear. All of this suggests that the character of faith is dependent upon the integrity of the gospel preached and that there is an intelligence that is indispensable for a workable faith.

As aforementioned, the presence of the Holy Spirit is no substitute for sound doctrine and sound minds. While our spirits are baptized, there is a need for baptized minds. This is spiritual intelligence.

Summary

*It is possible to be baptized in the Spirit and experience a deficit or lack of dimension of the Spirit being operative in the area of wisdom, revelation, discernment, and insight.

*The Holy Spirit enables our minds to comprehend the essence of the gospel and Scripture, but that doesn't guarantee that we will understand the application of its truths.

*The expression of our faith is dependent upon the integrity of gospel.

*There is an intelligence that is indispensable for a workable faith.

*The presence of the Holy Spirit doesn't mean we can't be misled.

*The Holy Spirit yields the power to understand the truth, but if what we're being taught is erroneous, that power is not beneficial.

4

EVIDENCE-BASED THEOLOGY

Theology is the science of faith. It represents human effort to interpret and encapsulate the Word of God into a useable and understandable form. Theology is, therefore, a *synthetic* product and not always divinely inspired or infallible. The operative word is synthetic. Only the Scriptures are original and retain the qualities of being inspired, trustworthy, and eternal (2 Tim. 3:16). Therefore, theology should always be open to scrutiny, and it should be secure enough to be challenged.

Ultimately, the testimony of its accuracy resides in its compliance with the Scriptures and in the character and behavior it produces in those who embrace it. Paul reminds Timothy of his own doctrine, manner of life, purpose, faith, longsuffering, charity, and patience (2 Tim. 3:10). The apostle clearly sets forth false concepts as one of the causes of immorality and unethical behavior (Rom. 1:16-32). Jesus said you shall know a tree by its fruit (Matt. 3:10; 7:17; Luke 6:44). The ultimate test of the profitability and validity of theology is the product it produces. Indeed, there can be appropriate doctrinal concepts without human compliance.

However, if theology truly reforms the spirit, mind and body; instills a consciousness of the true and living God; establishes Christ in the heart and mind; nurtures the best in human nature; stirs a sensitivity to the existence and needs of others; promotes personal responsibility and accountability; promotes growth and freedom; and delivers from oppression and exploitation of all kinds, then the evidence stands for itself. As such, truly making God known is evidence of sound theology.

Summary

*Theology is a human attempt to interpret the Word of God and surmise ideological themes related to life.

*Theology is not always divinely inspired, so it may be flawed. Thus, theology should always be open to scrutiny.

*Only the Scripture is original and retains the qualities of being inspired, trustworthy, and eternal.

*Theological accuracy is best evidenced in the character and behavior it produces.

*In order to make God known, the theology one embraces must be correct.

5

THEOLOGY OF AGING

Aging should be viewed as a reservoir of wisdom and understanding. Although the changes in our external appearance are not always synonymous with the internal reformation of thought, values, and priorities, a greater spiritual intelligence can develop with age. Paul writes to the Corinthians that although the outward man perishes, the inward man is renewed day by day (2 Cor. 4:16), developing into greater Christ-likeness.

In our contemporary culture, aging is often associated with retirement, compromised health, and social liabilities. Even in the presence of modern technology and health practices where rejuvenation and prolonged health are now options, aging has generally been viewed as a negative phase of life. The prophet Zechariah (8:4-5) made a most interesting pronouncement regarding the elderly in the Hebrew communities:

> *Thus says the LORD of hosts: 'Old men*
> *and old women shall again sit in the streets*
> *of Jerusalem, each one with his staff in his*
> *hand because of great age. The streets of the*

*city shall be full of boys and girls playing in
the streets.'*

This must be understood in a figurative sense as referring to long life and not taken to mean that men and women will be so feeble that they will need to walk with canes. As the prophet intimated, the presence of the elderly in a community is a sign of Divine grace and favor. The fact that war, child birth, sickness, and disease had not deprived a community of its repository of wisdom, knowledge, and intangible wealth is a visible token of Divine goodness.

There is neither a promise of an eternal existence in this time and space nor is there a complete exception from declining health. So we all will face declining health as we age and then eventually die. Nevertheless, the presence of the aged community should be seen as a potential resource to transform our thinking rather than a liability. When Paul exhorts us to put off the old man and put on the new, this is not a plea for an immediate external makeover but a transformation of thought, values, and objectives (Eph. 4:22-24). Renewal is in the inner consciousness, intuition, wisdom, knowledge, revelation, and inclination toward obedience to the Spirit, which occurs over time as we age.

During my years as chief of dentistry at a comprehensive health center, a group of us health providers came together to consider some alternative care for aging citizens in our community. We, at the time, had a "sandwich community," that is, adults with their own children who were also assuming responsibility for their aging parents. The team of healthcare providers came up with the idea of an adult day care services. There were day care facilities for children, so why not have one for the senior citizens who needed some form of managed care? The adult children would drop off their aging parents early in the morning and recover them in the evening just like they would for their small children. The idea worked and was a tremendous benefit.

In our local church, we organized programs that cared for people regardless of their age. We addressed many areas that relate to life ranging from children, youths, singles, married, divorced, and the elderly. We called our senior members the "super saints." It was an identification tag that promoted a rather different view of the aging population among us.

In a youth-oriented culture, we need to stop interpreting age by how young an old person appears. Youthfulness is not a respectful criterion for assessing the aging process. We can respect the abilities and limitations of our bodies while also honoring the wisdom and knowledge gained from our experiences. Perhaps the idea of a generation gap and the contemporary concepts of "old school" and "new school" may need to be re-examined for their correctness. Old school with new students may be the better paradigm.

Summary

*As our experience and knowledge increase with age, so, too, can our spiritual intelligence.

*There is a Biblical dimension to aging that needs to be re-examined.

*The presence of the elderly in a community is a blessing just as children are.

*A person's status should not be depreciated nor diminished simply because of age. In fact, greater respect is due the aged.

*There should be neither conflict nor competition between generations, but rather solutions to incorporate and enrich all members of a community.

*The elderly are to teach the young and the young should listen and grow in stature.

*The welfare and respect of the elderly should be common in the culture.

*Respect and honor of age has Biblical implications.

6

CULTURE OF SKEPTICISM

We live in a plural world of various ideas, thoughts, values, and perspectives. There is an acquired social intelligence that accommodates differences of opinions, especially when they are in conflict with our own. This is especially true regarding spiritual matters. The subtlety of any anti-Christian sentiment is to raise suspicion and even an intellectual skepticism regarding the reality of spiritual things. When doubt is masked as intelligence, then ignorance is called knowledge, fear is believed to be courage, and foolishness and presumption are thought to be faith. The consequence is rebellion to God and confusion.

From the beginning of creation, there has been a question about words and their meanings. The serpent asked the woman, "Hath God said?" The question did not intend to raise suspicion regarding the existence of God, but rather it sought to create a working skepticism regarding Divine words. This strategy of *creative skepticism* has been evident throughout the centuries in the form of theological debates and doctrinal disputes regarding the interpretation of the Bible. Liberal theologians and scholars have stumbled over such concepts as inerrancy and inspiration of Scripture. They have also expressed their confusion regarding alleged contradictions amidst some Biblical narratives.

We are living in a day of rational skepticism, dedicated doubt, intelligent ignorance, and unveiled rebellion and lawlessness. Progressivism and situational ethics are the prevalent tools of examining and excusing all forms of immorality and unethical behavior and character. It is alleged that there are no absolute truths; and that motives justify the actions regardless of their consequences. What was correct has now become incorrect and what was unacceptable has now become the norm. Every individual, it is alleged, is to judge what is best and correct for himself, and no one has the right to judge another. We have come to justify all personal efforts, lifestyles, and behavior based upon individual logic.

Supposedly, God is solely benevolent, and therefore, does not condemn anyone. Furthermore, if there are requirements for His love and blessings, then salvation is by works and not by grace. Some allege that our historical theological perspectives are incorrect and need adjustment. If we cannot solve new problems with the same logic and intelligence that created them, then it is alleged that foundations must be updated, reformed, and even dismissed. Such thinking raises suspicion that the architectural pattern for the universe is inaccurate. This rationale further suggests that the color spectrum may be incorrect; geometric measurements may be variable; life and death are myths; and perhaps you are simply a hologram of a million tiny particles superimposed upon a thin film of air. In fact, you may not really be reading this document at all. This growing myth of *relativism and constructed uncertainty* attempts to erode the concept of an eternal existence and an absolute reality.

Without God, man may do everything but accomplish nothing. When God ceases to speak to a person, then a fool exists. Death is a tragedy, but to be left alone without Divine intelligence is worse. The atheist believes God is simply a delusion while the agnostic acknowledges Divine existence but insists that it cannot be trusted. Many of us are *"conditionalists,"* for we believe and serve Him as long as there are incentives. However, Christianity is not incentive-driven. It is based on true faith, or knowing God, not on potential lifestyle benefits.

If the Bible is untrustworthy and is not really the inspired Word of God, then we have no accurate means to know of God, acknowledge His Son or respond to His Spirit. While we play with man's words and seek to challenge their meaning and relevance, creating constant skepticism and doubt, we must not do so with the unchanging Word of God found in the Bible. The knowledge of an eternal God and a resurrected Savior reside in the unchanging truths in the Scripture. Although the Scripture offers record of the nature and character of God and Divine involvement in human affairs, only the Holy Spirit can affirm the truth of our faith. Only through the Spirit, not ever-changing human intelligence, can we discover the truth and gain spiritual intelligence.

Summary

*When Divine revelation declines, human irrationality increases.

*There has always been an attempt to deceive by questioning the validity of words or statements, namely those of God.

*The strategy of *creative skepticism* has been to create a working skepticism regarding Divine words and the interpretation of a very historical text: the Bible.

*We are living in a day of rational skepticism, dedicated doubt, intelligent ignorance, and unveiled rebellion and lawlessness.

*Progressivism, intentionalism, and situational ethics are the prevalent tools of examining and excusing all forms of immorality and unethical behavior and character.

*Only the power of God can validate the truths of God.

*The Holy Spirit facilitates spiritual intelligence.

7

BIOSPIRITUALITY

The creation narrative recorded in the book of Genesis reveals God as Creator, Organizer, and Maintainer of all things (Gen. 1-3). It establishes the relationship between the Creator and the creation. "Biospirituality" is a term coined to express the reality that humanity (biology) is created in the image of God (spiritual).

The image of God is not a physical likeness but rather the endowment of faculties. These include rationality, creativity, dominion, righteousness, masculinity, femininity, and community. Rationality is the gift of intelligence and power to reason, communicate, and plan. Creativity is the capacity to make things and impart value to them. Dominion is the mastery over created things; control over the environment; ability to harness and manage the forces of nature; and capacity to establish cultures and civilization. Righteousness is the capacity to know the revealed will of God and to impart Divine preferences and values where life is concerned. Masculinity and femininity represent reproductive and social distinctions without restrictions of opportunities and privileges. Community is the capacity to live together in relationships.

While creation established the Divine-human connection, demonic deception and human rebellion separated this Creator-creature alliance (Gen.3:1-20). Humanity was not constituted to sin. Thus, sin is a contradiction to the original, created human nature, and God's original plan. The man and woman were created to live in righteousness. They were created to be and function as co-equal, co-essential, and co-substantial.

After man's choice to sin, God initiated a plan of recovery for humankind that is comprehensive (Gen. 17:1-9; Rom. 10:1-17). This salvation is the process through which God takes fallen humanity to its ultimate destiny. It is spiritual, psychological and behavioral. The spiritual dimension is represented in the process of regeneration, reconciliation, redemption, imputation, and sanctification. The psychological dynamic is the enabling of the human mind to receive and comprehend truth. The behavioral represents the strategies for human responses to such Divine revelation.

This Divine-human connection established in creation is restored in the salvation experience. Redeemed humanity, male and female, are delegated sovereigns. They are co-regents called to know God (John 17:3) and to make Him known in the earth (John 13:34-35). They are endowed with wisdom, knowledge, and understanding. They have redemption through His blood (Col.1:14) and access to God through prayer (Eph. 4:4-7). They are delivered from the power of evil and established in a sphere of reality that is superior to this present world (Col.1:13). They are no longer subject to generational curses or demonic possession. Spiritual intelligence enables us to comprehend the privileges, promises, and responsibilities of this great salvation.

We have the privileges of access to God through prayer; Spirit baptism and spiritual gifts and callings; deliverance from evil; guidance in life; and an understanding of spiritual things and how they relate to our lives. There are the promises of an eternal life; forgiveness of sin; and redemption through Jesus Christ. With this, we have the responsibility to live according to Divine guidelines and to bear witness of our redemption to others.

The crisis points of this Divine-human connection reside in the appearance of challenges in our personal lives and relationships. We must have spiritual intelligence to navigate through difficult times and recognize that God is not absent even when negative things are present. His grace, which is wisdom, knowledge and an internal confidence, will always be sufficient for us to overcome every obstacle and challenge regardless of its nature. He is not the author of our challenges, but He is the author and finisher of our faith (Heb. 12:2).

Summary

*Biospirituality maintains that humanity is created in God's image, being endowed with rationality, creativity, dominion, righteousness, and community.

*Humanity is not created to operate independently of Divine government, and worldliness is humanity seeking to govern itself without Divine guidance.

*Salvation through Christ restores the Divine-human connection.

*Salvation is the comprehensive process (spiritual, psychological, and behavioral) through which God takes the sinner from depravity to righteousness.

*Spiritual intelligence helps us to recognize our likeness to God and our need to rely on Him to overcome any challenge.

8

BIBLICAL PARADOXES

As redeemed people, we live our lives between two worlds of conflicting principles. One is seen and the other is unseen. The visible world consists of people, places, laws, institutions, and organizations seeking to govern itself without God. The invisible world is the Kingdom of God and is the realm of Divine government. The latter world is revealed in the teachings of Jesus. The principles of life that He advocated were in contradiction to those of the present world (Matt. 5:1-12, 20-22, 27-28; 6:33; John 18:36; 18:36; Luke17:21; 18:24). He spoke of a new citizenship that required a "born again" experience (John 3:1-21). His criteria for greatness was to serve others (Matt. 5:19; Luke 22:23-27), and true power and freedom was not experienced outward but inward (Matt. 6:33; 7:21; 11:11; 19:23-24; 21:31; Mark 7:21-23; 10:23-24; Luke 17:20-21). The apostolic writers set forth the idea of another world in which righteousness, peace, and joy were dependent upon a different set of values (Rom. 14:17; 2 Tim. 4:10; 1John 2:15-17). All of this expresses the idea of citizens living between two worlds that are in conflict. This fact becomes very clear when we consider the paradoxes in the Scriptures. A paradox is a tenet or principle that seems to contradict itself and is often contrary to common sense. For example, we are said to live in this world but we are not of this world (John 17:6-16).

The Bible is filled with such paradoxical statements that testify to the reality that the Kingdom of God is not of this world. It must be understood that the world is not houses, lands, mountains, rivers, and oceans. The world is humanity with all of its ideas, knowledge, wisdom, values, and institutions seeking to govern itself independently. In this context, the principles and values of the Kingdom are in contradiction to the status quo. For example, Matthew 10:39, asserts that we find our life by losing it. The operative phrase in the passage is "for My sake." We cannot afford the luxury of doing it our way, for God did not design humanity to operate independent of Divine involvement. Worldliness is humanity seeking to find itself and rule without God.

The God of the universe is willing to take over our lives. The critical question is: What do we lose or gain in allowing God to govern our lives? Is it an unhappy proposition to lose independency and find dependency? Humanistic determinism is the opposite of reliance on God. It is competing, warring and striving for preeminence. Meanwhile, Romans 12:1 exhorts us to present our bodies as living sacrifices to God which is our reasonable service. Reasonable means that it is the right thing to do.

Eyes to See

A dimension exists beyond this time and space that is limited to spiritual perception. Believers are endowed to see or perceive the unseen (2 Cor. 4:18). How is this possible? The natural man does not receive the things of God, for they are foolishness (1 Cor. 2:14). Hebrews says that redeemed people see Jesus crowned with glory (Heb. 2:9). Again, how is this possible for some and not for others? The Lord Jesus said that the Spirit would show us things of Him and things to come (John 16:13). Faith with spiritual intelligence allows believers to see beyond the obvious status of this present world and realize the God who holds all things in place.

What did Moses or Paul see? They saw the invisible and experienced the Divine. This is a mystery, which is a mystery is a truth or concept that is partly understood or that is understood by a select individual or group at a certain time and place. Paul records the essence of a mystery as something that was revealed to him and the apostles but was not made clear to those leaders under the old covenant (Eph. 3:1-12). Moses forsook the things of Egypt for things unseen for he perceived that true greatness resided in a different set of values and accomplishments (Heb. 11:24-27). Paul writes of a wisdom that is not understandable through natural reasoning (1 Cor. 2:5-16).

It requires a whole different group of faculties for redeemed humanity to know God. The book of Revelation has a phrase for consideration: "They that dwell upon the earth." (Rev. 3:10; 11:10; 13:8). Earth dwellers live for the earth and all its activities. As they age, they become more preoccupied with the demands and expectations of this world. However, spiritual intelligence enables the believer to perceive the true value beyond earthly limitations while maintaining a responsible citizenship in this present world.

Biblical Examples

The Scripture has many paradoxes. Spiritual intelligence provides us with an understanding of these paradoxes that is indispensable. It provides insight into the seemingly unknown and illogical so that we may be edified in our service to Christ. Let us example some of the most profound examples:

We must be born again to seek the Kingdom (John 3:3). All of us had a natural birth in order to see and experience the seen world, but we must have a spiritual rebirth with God as our Father in order to see and experience the unseen world. Once we are born again, we become part of a spiritual body called the Church, which is Christ's bride. Christ left His bride, the Church, on earth while he prepares a place for her. Thus, we are part of a supernatural Kingdom in which Christ rules now and forever. While on earth, our ideas and ideals should exemplify our citizenship in this Divine Kingdom.

Such a spiritual, psychological, and behavioral reformation can allow us to lay up treasures that are not seen and that do not perish (Matt. 6:19-21). It endows us with the capacity to perceive an unseen registry of our activities and objectives. Our beliefs and convictions do not come from the theology of this world but from the Scripture. This is the idea of paradoxes and the co-existence of two worlds.

We are exalted by being humble. According to Luke 14:11, "For whosoever exalts himself will be humbled, and he who humbles himself will be exalted." Psalms 75:6-7 declares that the power of promotion does not come from the east, the west or the south. God alone puts down one and exalts another. In this very competitive world, there may be a time to strive for preeminence by our own strength. However, there are times when such striving may run against the mandate of God. There is an intelligence that instructs us how to lean upon spiritual principles and precepts that are more powerful but seen outwardly to be foolish and weak.

Both Joseph and Daniel exercised influence while in bondage (Gen. 39-50; Dan. 1-12). Each of their situations demonstrated paradoxical principles. They were both in bondage, yet they revealed the powers of the Spirit. They had foresight to know times and seasons; discernment to predict change and proper response; and the ability to enlist the trust of others. If we humble ourselves and He exalts us, then we shall find the Joseph and Daniel sphere of influence. From these examples in scripture, we can conclude that self-assertiveness is not always productive. Rather, true humility always is because it is simple obedience to God.

We rest under a yoke. In Matthew 11:29-30, Jesus says to take my yoke, for it is easy. Everyone is under a yoke, or burden, of some form. It is either Divine or demonic. There is no rest or peace under the satanic yoke, for there are always wars and conflicts. However, Jesus said His yoke was just the opposite, a paradox. He was trying to make us understand that grace is a deliverance from the burden of the law. Salvation through faith in Him would be the new yoke that would actually lighten our load by delivering us from the power of sin. Jesus said to take His yoke and learn from Him. In fact, true faith is the emulation of Christ.

We conquer by yielding. Roman 13:14 exhorts us to yield to God, and sin will not overcome us. If we walk in the Spirit, then we will not fulfill the works of the flesh (Gal. 5:16). Prohibition accelerates desire. In other words, what we are forbidden to do actually puts the desire in our hearts and minds to do. However, if the compensation for obedience is greater, we will typically not do the forbidden. The compensation for our obedience is peace with God and eternal life. Furthermore, the Spirit compensates for our weakness, so if we yield to it, it will cause us to fulfill the will of God.

We are strong when we are weak. Tribulations produce perseverance (Rom. 5:3-4). Thus, a side-effect of challenges is an increase in character, such as determination, patience, hope and even understanding. Paul takes pleasure in challenges and difficulties, for when he is weak, then he is strong (2 Cor. 12:10). For the apostle declared that through him, Christ has revealed the power of salvation. The principle here is that weakness and strength must be redefined.

Weakness is neither complacency nor apathy, but it is reliance upon a different set of principles. For example, we may decide to wait on the Lord instead of trying to figure out something on our own. Waiting on the Lord is not passivity, though. In prayer, we put our situations in His hands, so we rely on His strength rather than ours. When we pray in tongues, for instance, the Holy Spirit makes intercession for us according to the will of God. The Spirit compensates for our ignorance and enables our mind to receive wisdom and knowledge of the Scriptures. Such revelation builds up our faith and confidence in the face of the most challenging circumstances.

We become great by becoming little. Matthew 18:3-4 says that he who behaves as a little child shall be great in the kingdom. We must be as trusting and humble as children in order to not only receive the message of the gospel, but also to live under its principle of unconditional love. Only then are we great in God's assessment, not when we make lots of money or become famous. There is an absolute need to be in touch with God, and our attitude must be child-like, relying totally on our Father. Remember, Jesus said the meek shall inherit the earth (Matt. 5:5).

Summary

*Paradoxes are statements or tenets that are contrary to popular beliefs.

*Biblical paradoxes express the difference between this world and the Kingdom of God.

*Spiritual intelligence enables a believer to comprehend t biblical paradoxes.

9

THE UNKNOWN GOD

Perhaps our understanding of God is the most significant challenge in our interpretation and integration of truth. There may be a discrepancy between the God of the Scripture and the various contemporary concepts and caricatures of the living God. Since there is a tendency to emulate what we worship, it is important to have an appropriate concept of God (Psalm 115:1-8; Rom. 1:20-32). Indeed, our intangible concepts, beliefs, and convictions become tangible when expressed through our lifestyles.

Paul's epistle to the Romans reveals a God that is personal (Rom. 1:7; 3:29-30; 8:14,16,17; 8:8, 31;14:17; 15:5, 13), moral (Rom. 2:4,11 8:7) , righteous (Rom. 1:17,18; 4:6 5:5;11:22, 29; 12:1) and unlimited (Rom. 4:17;5:10; 6:23;.11:33;13:1, 15:19). Contemporary theology presents a God that appears to be illusive, temperamental, indecisive, permissive, biased, and limited. In fact, the God of contemporary religious thought is oftentimes made to be synonymous with the doctrines, disciplines, and practices of the churches. It is not uncommon that the policies of the church demand the same allegiance and respect that is perhaps only due the Lord. This in no way discounts or discredits the validity and the necessity of doctrines, disciplines, and practices, but it expresses the danger of limiting and confusing the identity, person, character, and purposes of God with such expressions.

Human attempts to make the unknown God known include our own personal caricatures or views of God. For example, to some children and adults, God is the God of their parents or He is the excuse/compensation for human inability and frailty. He is the 'internal voice' that convicts you and makes you feel guilty when you make a mistake or you are unforgiving of others. He is that mystical source of peace and harmony in times of conflict and distress. He is like the parent that always demands perfection and obedience. He is source of traditions that seems to censor new ideas, new music, and new ways of doing things. He is the One who demands the tithe and attendance. He is the One who manages life and gives gifts, callings, careers, occupations, and even relationships. He is the One who engineers wars with evil forces and adversaries. He is the One who closes and opens doors. He is the pacifist who prohibits retaliation and retribution. He is the One who demands love and forgiveness of enemies and people who mean you harm. He is the God who makes conditional promises that are always based upon some human sacrifices of giving money or time. He is the One who seems not to ever be satisfied with human responses in worship unless it is emotional and ecstatic. He is the One who prunes, chastens, shakes, and tests you with unusual challenges, decisions, and options. He is the

One who seems to only speak through older people and leaders. He is the One who sometimes will let you down, disappoint you, and not answer your prayers. As startling as these caricatures may appear to some, they represent only a brief summary of human perceptions of a loving God who cares for His children.

Sovereignty

God actions are often perceived without an understanding of His ways or nature. For example, it is possible to regard Him as the source of healing, deliverance, guidance, and miracles, and not comprehend the nature of the power and grace behind these great demonstrations. That may be the reason why such perplexity arises when these displays of Divine privileges are not equally shared with the same predictability among all believers. Indeed, all of these manifestations of power are under the absolute sovereignty of God. Perhaps, the reason that some are healed, delivered, and restored and some are not, may reside in the fact that such supernatural powers are signs that point us to a greater reality. Even when these benefits are not equally shared by all who expect them, they serve a greater purpose of provoking faith and a consciousness of an age or realm to come.

Our concept of God is often confused by the co-existence of good and evil, as revealed in the parable of the tares and wheat (Matt. 13:24-30). God is sovereign and rules over all times, seasons and circumstances. He has given humanity the freedom to choose between good and evil. The parable reveals the sources of the problem as being the devil and humankind. Evil permeates the world with all of its systems, government, and institutions because the human powers that should be governing with righteousness are asleep or preoccupied with lesser issues. It must also be remembered that when humanity rebels against God, it subjects itself to Satanic and demonic influence. For in the beginning all creation, the earth and creatures were designed to function according to Divine plans. Rebellion introduced all forms of disease, disorder, disorganization, and disaster into the world.

In addition to the whole question of evil in the world, we desire God to see our enemies as His own. Nevertheless, He does not deal with them in a manner that is quite to our liking. In fact, we are instructed to forgive those who abuse and persecute us (Matt. 6:14-15). We prefer to interact with people who are like ourselves in behavior, value, and conduct, yet God is not exclusive. God seemingly interacts with people who do not demonstrate His character and values. At times, we are perplexed over His mercy and His desire for salvation rather than condemnation (Jonah 4:1-11; Mark 16:16). Perhaps God extends time for repentance even for those who willingly disobey. After all, it is not His will that any should perish but that all come to the knowledge of the truth (2 Peter 3:9). Paul sums up this controversy with a wonderful statement in the epistle to the Romans:

> *O the depth of the riches both of the wisdom and knowledge of God! How unsearchable are His judgments and His ways past finding out!* (Rom. 11:33)

God still provides creative ideas, concepts, and even organization to reconcile estranged and confused humanity to Himself. Laws, legislation, and concepts of righteousness are revelation of a loving God. It is amazing that in a world that is operating on wrong principles and seeks to govern itself without His rules, that God still imparts models of righteousness to counteract all forms of evil. Consider the reconciliation movements that sought to eliminate conflict between racial, ethnic, and national groups. In fact, every revival is an extension of grace in the form of instruction and correction of the mistakes of humanity.

Faith

Even the ideas of faith in the unknown God poses controversy. Although the Lord is all powerful and can do anything, there are some things that He will not do because of His own self-imposed restrictions. In creation, He delegated power to the man and woman to reason, rule, create, and reproduce. These delegated abilities can function without supernatural intervention.

Faith comes by hearing and accepting propositions (Rom. 10:17). For example, if we come to God, then we must believe that He is God and that He rewards our diligent efforts to obey Him (Heb. 11:6). In essence, God responds to human obedience to His will, yet He deals with ignorance and rebellion differently. While ignorance may precipitate disobedience, rebellion is disobedience with knowledge. An individual may act inappropriately because of lack of information. However, to consistently live contrary to established Biblical norms provokes a different response. Jesus asked the Pharisees if they understood His teaching (Matt. 22:41-46; Mark 12:35-40; Luke 21:39-44). Their response provoked a judgment because they claimed that they understood, yet they chose to disobey. Spiritual illumination is given to those who are ignorant while spiritual blindness is allowed in those who continually walk in rebellion (Rom. 11:25).

Prayer

Even the privilege of prayer creates some controversy. Even though His "yoke is easy and His burden is light," this process of communion is often confused. Prayer is not warfare even though there are several Scriptural references that are used to convey this concept (2 Cor. 10:4-5; 1 Cor. 9:26; Gal. 4:19; Eph. 6:10-19). War is given to such scriptural references as "travail with birth pangs," "wrestling," and "prevailing in the night seasons." Even the example of Daniel praying to get through to the Lord is used to justify this concept of wrestling and battling (Gen. 32:24-32; Dan. 10:12-14). Occasionally prayer is even described as the process through which the Lord is persuaded to respond. In such cases, the believer verbally rehearses numerous Scripture before the Lord in an effort to remind Him of His promises. However, prayer is no substitute for human responsibility. God will not do what He has empowered His children to do.

The confusion is further accentuated by the alleged indecisiveness of the Lord in which a request may receive the answer of yes, no, maybe or wait. The record of Paul's pleading with the Lord three times to remove his thorn in the flesh and the Lord's refusal to do so is often used as the validation of this position (2 Cor. 12:7-9). In spite of the fact that Jesus says, "Ask anything in My name, and I will do it," and "When you pray, believe that you receive it, and you shall have it," it is taught that unanswered prayer is to be expected. Once again, Divine liability will not take the place of human responsibility. Whatever He has delegated and empowered us to do, He will not do Himself.

Judgment

The perplexity of prayer is further accentuated by the belief that God randomly chastens, prunes, and purges His children. It is certain that the "wages of sin" is death, and the principle of sowing and reaping declares that if you commit a fault, there are consequences (Gal. 6:7). As a result, it is assumed that the Lord sets in motion a series of processes to strengthen the faith, endurance, and authority of the believer. The book of Psalms has been used to substantiate such claims. Consider some of the references:

Thou hast proved mine heart; thou hast visited me in the night; thou hast tried me, and shall find nothing; I am purposed that my mouth shall not transgress (17:3).

For thou, O God, hast proved us; thou hast tried us, as silver is tried (66:10).

The book of Job is also used as the foundation of these presuppositions (1:6-12). It is interesting that nowhere in the analysis of the text is there any indication that the calamities were orchestrated by the Lord. The challenges were initiated by Satan to prove the premise that faith toward God is incentive-driven. Satan asserts Job's faithfulness is based upon the benefits he receives. Even though the apostle James writes that God neither proves nor tempts anyone with evil (James 1:13), there are beliefs in our contemporary faith community that the negative encounters and difficulties that believers experience in their world are for the sake of spiritual exercise. Consequently, the Lord is supposed to provide the administration of such forms of discipline that may include the loss of relationships, jobs, possessions, and even health. Even church splits are attributed to the "purging of the Lord." While misbehavior has its consequences, God is the author of our faith and not the author of any temptations or intentional harm.

Make no mistake, God, who is Holy and demands obedience, is a judge. Therefore, he must judge sin. He judged Adam and Eve, dispelling them from the Garden (Gen. 3). Similarly, throughout the Old Testament, He judged the Israelites for their disobedience and lack of loyalty in serving idols. He allowed them to be captured and enslaved by the Babylonians and Assyrians. God's judgment even fell on children who mocked the prophet Elisha (2 Kings 2:23-25). In the New Testament, He judged Ananias and Sapphira for lying to the Spirit (Acts 5:1-10), as well as the Corinthians for defiling the Lord's Supper (1 Cor. 11:29-32). Furthermore, a day of judgment is promised for us all (Matt. 12:36-37; Acts 17:31; James 5:9), but ultimately, true believers will not be condemned to eternal separation from God.

Delegation

The idea of delegated authority is supposed to represent the privilege given to a select group who are called to rule and represent Divine interests, concerns, and judgments (Heb. 13:17; 1 Pet. 3:1; Acts 20:17-37). Indeed, gifts and callings are given to the Church to equip the saints for the work of the ministry (Eph.

4:11-12), but leaders are given to empower the saints and not to dominate nor oppress them. After all, this is the admonition of Paul to the Ephesian elders that they take heed to themselves and to the congregation which the Holy Ghost has made them overseers (Acts 20:28).

Propitiation

Even though the Lord freely gives to His children all things, it is alleged that some of these blessings are conditional and require a sacrificial donation. While there is the admonition to give and it shall be given unto you, this is often interpreted to mean that spiritual blessings can be precipitated by financial donations. Once again, it is more blessed to give than to receive, but God should not be mistaken as a pagan god who demands propitiation through gifts and sacrifice. The prophet Elijah mocked the people who worshipped pagan gods, saying, "Cry aloud, for he is god; either he is meditating or he is busy…" (1 Kings 18:27). Pagan gods are temperamental and erratic and always given benefits in response to human sacrifices of some kind. God is not a pagan, and to claim that His blessings are precipitated by sacrifices of any kind is contrary to Scripture and His nature as sovereign. A degree of spiritual intelligence is needed to navigate through this very sensitive area.

Equality

It is alleged in some faith communities that the Lord chooses only His sons instead of His daughters to rule in His kingdom. Words such as "head," "covering," "submission," "silence," and "authority" are used to substantiate this position of male election and female subjection. Yet, the Scripture declares that, in Christ, there is neither male nor female (Gal. 6:15; Col. 3:11). Furthermore, there are distinct references in the Scripture to women leaders such as Deborah, Huldah, Sarah, Junia, Tryphena, Tryphosa, Julia, Priscilla, Phoebe, Lydia, and the "Elect Lady and her children" (2 John 1:1). God is reportedly still angry with Eve for her being deceived and for her disobedience, so He continues to administer punishment upon all women in the form of submission, subjection, painful childbirth, and work restrictions. This discussion is explored extensively under the chapter titled "A Justification for Abuse."

His Dwelling

Another misrepresentation of God is that he lives in our church buildings. In fact, we even call the building "House of God." However, God does not dwell in buildings made with hands or is He limited to any specific place, certain geographic locations. There are no spiritual centers or religious buildings that can be regarded as the houses of God (Acts 18:24-25). His presence is not enhanced through the construction of a physical temple where certain types of music, songs, and dances are used for the celebration of His glory. It is interesting that most of the ceremonies for the dedication of buildings use Old Testament references (Exodus 30:26, 40:9; Lev. 8:10; Num. 7:1). The New Testament makes it clear that the dwelling place of God is among and in redeemed people (John 14:17; 1 Cor.3:16; 6:19). In fact, we are the Church, the body of believers called unto God through Christ.

Revelation

As aforementioned, knowledge must be added to faith for spiritual intelligence. This is especially true when we consider the concept of progressive revelation. For example, the Old Testament is revealed in the New Testament, and the New Testament is concealed in the Old Testament. Truths are often concealed in types and symbols in the Old Testament but disclosed in the New Testament (Heb. 4-10). Paul expresses this principle of progressive revelation as a mystery (Eph. 3:1-3). Even though the truths of God may be concealed in types and symbols and later revealed and fulfilled, there is no indication that Divine precepts are to be open for re-interpretation by each succeeding generation of believers. His truths endure from one generation to another. There are no variations in the ethical and moral requirements of the Lord. Once again, spiritual intelligence enables us to understand the things that are timeless (changeless) and those that are timely (changeable).

Consequences of Believing but Not Knowing Him

As common and as extraordinary as some of these caricatures of the identity, purposes, acts, and ways of God may appear, they represent a subtle crisis in Christianity today. The known God may be very unknown to many believers. Perhaps we have created a mental concept of the Lord that limits our communion with Him and restricts His influence and direction in our lives.

There is a possibility that Paul draws upon this connection between the revelation of God and human character and behavior in the epistle to the Romans (1:20-30). He concludes that when Israel no longer retains the true knowledge of God in their consciousness, there is degeneration of their character. Paul attributes the loss of Israel's moral, ethical and reproductive character to the fact that they "changed the glory of the incorruptible God into an image made like corruptible man and birds and four-footed beast and creeping things" (Rom. 1:23). Because they "exchanged the truth of God for the lie, and worshipped and served the creature rather than the Creator," God gave them over to vile passions (Rom. 1:24-31).

As previously noted, there is an incarnation of beliefs into reality. When the true knowledge of the identity, character, and ways of the Lord are confused and even lost, there is a subsequent degeneration of the attitude, behavior, and character of the people. They emulate degeneracy and not holiness.

As aforementioned, Paul calls Him the "God and Father of our Lord Jesus Christ," "the Father of mercies" and "God of all comfort." The description of Him being the "God of all comfort" is a most unusual characterization of the Lord (2 Cor. 1:3). Comfort is applied to situation and circumstances of distress, disaster, crisis, disappointment, disillusionment, devastation, failure, and every conceivable dimension of human impotence, loss, pain, and suffering. He is the God of "all comfort" and is the sovereign Lord over all the consequences of evil. Comfort must then include correction and restoration; it must make the "crooked straight and the rough plan;" it must of necessity heal and deliver; it must reconcile and recover; it must give a different perspective to history; and it assuredly must provide hope for the future. If sin is the disruption, distortion, discomfort, disqualification, and the annulment of all creation, then the God of all comfort is the God of consolation and is the One who presides over all discomfort. For after all, Paul writes that God "comforts us in all our tribulation, that we may be able to comfort those who are in any trouble, with the comfort with which we ourselves are comforted by God" (2 Cor. 1:3-4).

For Paul, whenever believing people lose consciousness of the God of all comfort, they are troubled with fear, anxiety, distress, hopeless, and despair. With their minds, they conceive ideas, thoughts, imaginations, devices, strategies, schemes, and judgments that make them vulnerable to self-destructive patterns of behavior that contradict their redemptive status (1 Tim. 4:1-3; 2 Tim. 4:3-4). In other words, some know about God, but they don't know Him. If they knew God, their actions and reactions would be that of faith, peace, joy, self-control, and love, or the fruit of the Spirit (Gal. 5:22-23).

Since we emulate what we worship, it is important that our individual conceptions of Divine power and authority are compatible with the truths of Scripture (Rom. 1:20-32).

Summary

*A discrepancy exits between the God of the Scripture and the various contemporary concepts and caricatures of the living God.

*The God of contemporary religious thought is oftentimes made to be synonymous with the doctrines, disciplines, and practices of the churches.

*Since we typically emulate what we worship, we must have an appropriate concept of God.

*Acts of God are often experienced without an understanding of His ways.

*The sovereignty of God is neither subject to human faith nor beliefs.

*Human expression in the worship experience should not be confused with Divine presence.

*God does not dwell in temples and churches. Instead, He dwells among and in us.

*The truths of God endure throughout every generation.

* Spiritual intelligence is needed in order to know God.

II
MAKING HIM KNOWN

10

SPIRITUAL EQUILIBRIUM

Spiritual equilibrium is an expression of Divine purposes, priorities, and perspectives for all of creation, including human compliance to Divine directives. We must work toward a balance between thought, ideas and proper behavior. Spiritual concepts, such as beliefs and convictions, are expressed in natural and conceptual ways. As such, we will see that there are symptoms of spiritual imbalance that are expressed in our lives.

While the salvation of the individual may be the center of the Divine will, it is not the circumference. For example, Scripture indicates that the earth shall be filled with the glory and knowledge of the Lord (Hab. 2:14). In other words, human salvation is a portion of a comprehensive salvation that encompasses all earthly things. Spiritual equilibrium involves understanding this concept and the relationship that exists between spiritual concepts, such as beliefs and convictions, and natural characteristics, such as attitude and behavior. In essence, spiritual issues often express themselves in natural ways.

The Holy Spirit helps facilitate this spiritual equilibrium. The Holy Spirit is the executive agent of the Trinity and mediates all interaction between the heavenly and earthly spheres. The Holy Spirit is received as power and not intelligence. The intelligence of God is to be found in the Scripture. The Holy Spirit enables our minds to comprehend salvific truths but does not inform our minds intellectually. Consequently, the presence of the Holy Spirit is no substitute for sounds minds and sound concepts. In fact, the nine gifts of the Holy Spirit should be complemented by a tenth gift: common sense. We are rational creatures and should use the mind and will to engage sound ideas and judgment.

Sound ideas and judgment will flow from a person who walks in faith and spiritual equilibrium. However, the interpretation and integration of biblical truths into our lives has always been the crisis of our faith, creating a spiritual imbalance or discord among believers. Paul recorded this very prevalent danger in his epistles to the Romans (1:16-32; 3:1-31), Corinthians (15:12-29; 11:1-20; 13:1-5), Galatians (1:6-12; 3:1-29), Ephesians (1:16-19; 2:1-5), Colossians (1:19-20) and Hebrews (5:12-14; 6:1-3). The Ephesians received the Holy Spirit as power but lacked the intelligence necessary for balance and equilibrium. The Galatians could not sustain the reality of the Law as a schoolmaster and accept another gospel. The Corinthians expressed their lack of understanding of spiritual matters in their lawlessness, factions and heresies. The Hebrew epistle expressed the idea of sustained immaturity and an inability to progress from types and symbols to realities. The Colossians were guilty of mixing and adding strange elements to their faith. Peter exhorts the saints to add knowledge to their faith, indicating that convictions can be deficient of understanding (2 Pet, 1:4-8). Paul exhorts Jude to contend for the faith once delivered to the fathers (Jude 1:3-4).

Individuals and churches that have an improper, imbalance concept of faith, that is, a lack of equilibrium, will demonstrate fanaticism, sensationalism, presumption, and irrationality. Real faith, on the other hand, expresses Divine liability but also human responsibility. That is, faith demands that we know what God will and will not do. He will not do what He has empowered us to do and neither will He repeat what is deemed a finished process. Human responsibility becomes very clear once we recognize our own boundaries. Failure to do so often degenerates into complacency, apathy, and irrationality.

In our contemporary faith culture, lack of spiritual equilibrium is expressed in strife, competition, factions, divisions, and all forms of ethical and moral failures. Gender oppression and racial strife is a loss of spiritual orientation due to misconception of Scripture. A classic premise and lack of balance is the belief that confession alone will correct what behavior has created. That is, the verbal pronouncements of Bible verses and promises alone will not correct that which demands an attitudinal and behavioral response. This premise can be expressed in any sphere of human existence.

Spiritual equilibrium, like physical wellness, has indicators. Blood pressure, weight, and heart rate will tell you something about physical wellness. Purpose, perspective, and priorities will tell you about spiritual equilibrium. Purpose speaks of proper orientation to essential function, gifting, and calling. Perspective expresses a healthy assessment of the issues of life and their interrelationship. Priority is the order of importance, significance, value, respect, honor, and condition.

The following are possible symptoms of imbalance:
*competition and strife
*disorientation and depression
*distinction based upon gender, race, age, socioeconomic status
*preoccupation with either the spiritual at the expense of doctrine or vice versa
*warfare concepts that produce compulsive behavior patterns
*overspecialization in aspects of the gospel
*pulpit-centered worship
*heavy authority, domination, undue opposition to change
*generation gap conflicts

Faith is a comprehensive word into which other words correspond, including patience, endurance, practicality, integrity, and love. Each of these words and others express human responses to Divine promises and privileges. They demonstrate the power of choice, creativity, imagination, memory, rationality, and as aforementioned, balance, and equilibrium.

Sound judgment will flow from a person who walks in faith

and spiritual equilibrium. Faith is not a denial of reality but the recognition of finality. Faith does not deny the existence of facts, circumstances, or even people, but it does acknowledge that God has the last word. That is, faith enables us to look beyond the obvious. While it does not permit us to escape the realities and challenges of life, it does open the door to possibility.

Spiritual equilibrium is expressed in the concept of sanctification as a comprehensive process that involves the spirit, soul, and body. Well-being, from a Biblical perspective, includes a salvation experience, redemptive consciousness, and behavioral reformation. Salvation is deliverance from the power of sin and all of its consequences. It also involves the restructuring of the attitude and behavior of the believer.

Spiritual equilibrium expresses the relationship between beliefs, convictions and behavior. It is the balance you gain by proper assessment of Divine intentions, thoughts, and precepts, which is seen in one's purpose, priority, and perspective.

Summary

*Spiritual equilibrium is a manifestation of spiritual intelligence.
*Spiritual equilibrium represents human compliance to Divine directives.
*The Holy Spirit is received as power to comprehend salvation truths, not the intelligence needed to interpret and adapt principles found in the Scriptures.
*The presence of the Holy Spirit is no substitute for sounds minds and concepts.

*An improper concept of faith is a spiritual imbalance and is often expressed in fanaticism, sensationalism, presumption, and irrationality.

*Faith demands that we know what God will and will not do.

11

REDEMPTIVE CONSCIOUSNESS

Redemptive consciousness is associated with spiritual equilibrium and expresses the connection between thoughts and behavior. As aforementioned, words and ideas are the catalysts for attitudes and behaviors. Thoughts eventually influence our perceptions of ourselves and even our world. This is especially true of words, ideas, and thoughts that have a Biblical origin. Of particular interest is the word "redemption," which is often used in our culture.

Redemption carries the meaning of change, deliverance, freedom, and even opportunity. From a Biblical perspective, redemption is one of the words that define the salvation process. Salvation is the comprehensive process by which God takes the sinner from depravity to a new destiny in Christ. It is a word into which several words fit, including justification, regeneration, reconciliation, sanctification, imputation, and propitiation.

While salvation provides for the deliverance, forgiveness, restoration, healing, and recovery of the individual, redemption is that aspect of the salvation process that defines a new image and status. This change is not self-initiated or is it individually navigated. It is a Divine initiative. It is neither by works nor compliance to a set of rituals or legislations. It is an expression of a Divine strategy and grace for the recovery of the individual. It is not religious, but it is Christian. Therefore, it cannot be explained or expressed outside of the context of the finished work of Jesus Christ, the initiating work of gospel, and the perpetual work of the Holy Spirit.

While the source of redemption is Divine, the benefits and privileges of the process are often expressed in human vocal proclamations, such as mottos. In this study, we shall examine various terms, phrases and proverbial sayings that find their origins in this idea of redemption.

Mottos

A motto, or slogan, is a phrase selected to provide an identity to an individual or organization. For example, when applied to a church, it describes the emphasis, theme or even specialty of the church. Consider the following:

*Friendly Church
*Worshipping Church
*Healing Church
*Deliverance Church
*Church of All People and Nations
*Kingdom Church
*Prophetic Church

*Apostolic Church
*A Place to Belong

Idioms

Idioms are expressions that state something figuratively that can be taken literally but shouldn't be. Sometimes we use them to soften the expression or to be kind to someone. Consider the following:

*I'm going to hit the sack
*I'm in hot water
*I'm up in the air
*Blow my top
*Lose your marbles
*Hot under the collar
*In a pickle/jam
*I went out on a limb
*Paid an arm and a leg
*Put a bug in your rear
*Get off my back
*Chip on your shoulder
*Starving to death
*Could eat a horse

Biblical Idioms

The Bible even has some idioms that have been commonly used. Consider the following:

*God owns the cattle on a 1,000 hills. This means that God owns it all, the planet and everything on it.

*Scepter shall not depart from Judah. This means a king will always hail from the lineage (tribe) of Judah.

*Beware of dogs. This means to avoid gossips and troublemakers.

*Wells without water. This means false teachers.

*Dog returns to his own vomit. This means a person who repeats his mistakes.

*Thorn in the flesh. This means a grievance or problem.

*Make a noise like a dog. This means to threaten but do nothing.

Hyperbole

The Bible contains figures of speech that are often an exaggeration to make or reinforce a point. Consider the following:

*It is easier to pass through the eye of needle than for a rich man to enter the kingdom (Luke18:25). Due to conflicting allegiances and material reliance, this makes it extremely difficult but not impossible for the wealthy.

*If anyone comes to me and does not hate father and mother, his wife and children, and brethren, and sisters, yea, and his own life also, he cannot be my disciple (Luke14:26). This means to put Christ first or make His aims a priority.

*If your right eyes cause you to sin, gouge it out and throw it away, for it is better to lose one part of your body than for whole body to be cast into hell (Matt. 5:29). This means that totally abstaining, denying or restricting oneself is better than falling into deadening sin due to living liberally, which grace affords the believer.

Redemptive Expressions

Now let us examine a few redemptive expressions that are derived from the Scripture. These sayings or proverbs are short and concrete expressions of a truth based upon common sense or practical experience.

*God is for us
*Jesus Christ, the same yesterday, today, and forever
*God knows
*He is Lord
*Plead the blood of Jesus
*I rebuke you, Satan
*Pulling down strongholds
*Waiting for a breakthrough
*Standing on the promises
*Going through
*Praying through
*Pray my strength in the Lord
*Waiting on the Lord
*He is my Jehova Jireh, my provider
*The will of the Lord be done
*Standing in faith and believing
*No weapon formed against me will prosper
*Standing on His word
*Let go and let God
*Cast all your cares on Him
*By His stripes, I am healed
*He shall supply all my needs

*He is my help and strength

*This is the day the Lord has made

*Be strong in the Lord

*Put on the whole armor

*Fight the good fight of faith

*Looking to God

There are of course many other such sayings that can be derived from the Scripture. To embrace these ideas and thoughts contributes to a consciousness of one's redemption that causes us to be more Christlike and victorious through Him. Spiritual intelligence helps us to understand, adapt and employ the figurative expressions in the Bible to glorify God and edify our lives.

Summary

*Redemptive consciousness explains the connection between thought and behavior for the believer.

*Words and ideas are the catalysts for our attitudes and behaviors.

*Thoughts eventually influence our perceptions of ourselves, others and the world.

*We must understand the figurative expressions used in the Bible, so that we have greater understanding of their intent and purpose.

*The deeper understanding needed to comprehend and adapt the figurative statements in the Bible, comes from spiritual intelligence.

*Redemptive expressions can shape our attitude.

12

SPIRITUAL INTEGRATION

The term "integration" has traditionally been used in association with civil rights, specifically public schools. However, the term can also relate to any joining or mixing of items and elements that can go together. For example, the re-establishment of certain concepts, ideas, or viewpoints existing in areas of faith can also be described as "integrated."

There are conceptual relationships that exist within the Scriptures. Such associations are referred to as integrations. When these integrations are disrupted, significant consequences occur. This can be seen when there is an imbalance or disassociation between Word/Spirit; Old Covenant/New Covenant; Church/Kingdom of God; spirituality/practicality; supernatural/natural; sacred/secular; crucifixion/resurrection; creation/fall; gifts-callings/sanctification; heavenly/earthly; male/female; and other crucial relationships. For example, the disassociation between Word and Spirit can affect the character of one's faith. All Word and no Spirit results in dead intellectuality, and all Spirit and no Word degenerates into fanaticism. When the work and mission of the church is separated from an understanding of the Kingdom of God, then there is a priority on individual salvation rather than upon stewardship of our communities. And of course, if gifts and callings are void of integrity (sanctification), then the longevity and effectiveness of a ministry will be shortened.

The segregation of any of the above relationships can serve as the catalyst for some very non-productive behavioral patterns. Just as segregation defines separation and even unequal privileges and rights in the sociopolitical sphere, the same term expresses the havoc that occurs when delicate integrations are not maintained in areas of faith. So spiritual integration defines the re-association of conceptual relationships and the restoration of a proper balance.

Spiritual integration is the re-uniting of faith and reliance upon God with human endeavors. Consider the fact that theology is the science of faith. It is human effort, hopefully inspired, to interpret and encapsulate an inspired record. Science is a descendant of faith and should stay close to its parent. When science, expressed as medicine and technology, becomes separated from faith, then a variety of dysfunctions arise. Humanity loses the consciousness of God and seeks to govern itself. It credits all of its advancements to itself. The consequences of such behavior are catastrophic.

Therefore, human wholeness must have an integrated approach that encompasses spirit, mind and body. Included in that must be economics, science, education, government athletics, entertainment, and religion. There must be the recognition of the purposes and intention of God for all creation. Likewise, there must be the reality that human creativity and rationality cannot function effectively without the knowledge and honor of the Divine source of all things.

Consider the relationships between the following:

*Word and Spirit
*The young and the old
*Carnality and spirituality
*Gifts and callings
*Church and Kingdom of God
*Sacred and secular
*Past, present, and future
*Creation and the Fall
*Reconciliation and salvation
*Justification and sanctification
*Spiritual man and natural man
*Crucifixion and resurrection
*Spirit and soul
*Spirituality and practicality
*Supernatural and natural
*Heavenly and earthly
*Science and faith
*Acquired and inherited
*Divine interaction and human response
*Divine liability and human responsibility
*Spirit, soul, and body
*faith and work

*Thought and behavior
*Common sense and spiritual sense
*Faith and medicine
*Age and health
*Natural and supernatural
*Imagination and reality
*Love and marriage
*Behavior and motivation
*Sowing and reaping
*Friends and enemies
*Protestant, Catholic, and Pentecostal
*The Gospel and the Law

Spiritual integration is the re-uniting of faith with reliance upon God with human endeavors. Spiritual intelligence is gained when these healthy relationships are established and maintained.

Summary

*Spiritual integration is the re-establishment of divergent but interdependent concepts, ideas or viewpoints that exist in areas of faith.
*There are conceptual relationships that exist within the Scriptures referred to as "tensions." When these tensions are disrupted, imbalanced or disassociated, there are significant potentially catastrophic consequences.
*Spiritual integration also involves the re-uniting of technology (human endeavors) and faith (reliance upon God).
*Science is a child of faith and should stay close to its parent.

When science, expressed as medicine and technology, becomes separated from faith, then a variety of dysfunctions arise.

13

A JUSTIFICATION FOR ABUSE

Can the Bible be misused to justify hurting certain people and reinforce destructive behavior, namely against women? Are there certain religious beliefs that relate to the abuse of women? Can extreme doctrines of male headship and female submission put an individual, family or even a congregation at a risk of abuse?

Many of the traditional religious concepts of male dominance, and female submission and inferiority correlate with some of the reasons behind abuse in the marriage and family. There is no suggestion that any of these beliefs alone necessarily causes abuse. However, the concern is whether these beliefs can interact with other factors and create an atmosphere where abuse may occur. Beliefs and convictions have tremendous consequences upon social behavior, and since our beliefs and convictions are predicated in the Word of God, we must examine it to determine the origin and influence of the misconceptions about marriage and family roles.

Main Topics and Texts

The primary passages from which interpretations are taken regarding women are 1 Corinthians 11 and 14; 1 Timothy 2; Colossians 3; Ephesians 5; and 1 Peter 3. According to authors Kroeger and Beck in "Women, Abuse, and the Bible: How Scripture Can Be Used to Hurt or to Heal," these passages are traditionally interpreted in the following manner:

1. Creation order is a God-ordained hierarchy that places the man above the woman in authority in marriage and the family. The husband is the head, the leader (priest), and the authority over the wife and children, with the wife only having authority over the children. Final authority in all matters always belongs to the husband or the man.

2. Marriage offers specific roles for the husband and the wife. The role of the leader belongs to the husband who is responsible for the spiritual welfare of the family, and the wife is the submissive member.

3. The husband and wife may discuss major decisions, but the final power of decision rests with the husband.

4. The role of providing for the family belongs to the husband while the internal affairs of the home, such as raising the children, belongs to the wife.

5. The term *patriarchy* is used to describe the social organization and the set of beliefs that grant and sustain male dominance over women and children.

The male-female submission issues in biblical interpretation relates primarily to five topics and texts:

1. The meaning of the term *kephale* or "head" (1 Cor. 11:2-16 and Eph. 5:21-33).
2. The meaning of *authentein* or "authority over" (1 Tim. 2:12 and 1 Tim. 2:8-15).
3. The creation order relationship of men and women taken from Genesis 1-3.
4. The Old Testament passages that reveal women in authority and the passages that relate women in the life of Jesus and within the ministry of Paul's circle of leaders (Matt. 9:20-22; Luke 7:36-50, 10:38-42; John 4:28-29, 39, 42; Rom. 16:1, 3, 7, 12).
5. The meaning of "submission and silence" in 1 Corinthians 14:34-35.

Beliefs on Authority and Their Implications

There are at least four religious views regarding the issue of authority. They are as follows:

1. The Old Testament supports male leadership and views the example of Deborah and the few prophetesses as exceptions to the norm. The phrase in Genesis 3:16 that "he shall rule over thee" is taken literally as a mandate of God for succeeding generations. This traditional view supports the exclusive male headship and female submission since "the head of the woman is the man" (1 Cor. 11:3). It prohibits

women from teaching men, for instance (1 Tim. 2:12; Titus 2:3-4), because the man was created first. This has established a dependency of the woman on the man; and because, in Genesis 2:23, the man named the woman, that has also established male authority.

2. The male leadership view allows women to teach but not to hold positions of authority. Its foundation is rooted in the belief that the Fall is the result of the mistake of the sexes exchanging their distinctive position and function, with the woman taking the lead. Nevertheless, Genesis 1 and 2 stresses the complementary relationship of men and women and does not indicate the inferiority of women. Genesis 2 does establish a difference in function but not status.

3. The plural view stresses equality because of redemption and the new creation but acknowledges the existence of functional differences related to the man and the woman. Both are divinely designed for specific roles that cannot be interchanged regardless of any exceptions. The man's role as leader and provider is as significant as the woman's role as nurturer and caretaker of the home.

4. The egalitarian view stresses the full equality of men and women in the church without distinction. Men and women can lead and exercise authority under all circumstances. Redemption and the new creation establish the co-essential, co-equal, and the co-substantial status of the man and the woman. (Clouse and Culver, 1989)

The positions taken by some of the Church Fathers influence contemporary thought. A collection of writing written near the end of the 1st and the beginning of the 2nd centuries by authors who were thought to be apostles of Jesus, or at least represent the thinking of the apostles, makes up the compilation titled "The Church Fathers." The writings are usually addressed to churches, or members of the church, and treat specific needs or problems. They make frequent references to Scripture and insist that they be in complete harmony with the gospel teaching. A few of their views on women are most interesting:

"Man is strong, active, uncastrated, mature; woman is weak, passive, castrated, immature" (Marcovich, 2002).

"It is not proper for a woman to speak in church, however admirable or holy what she says may be, merely because it comes from female lips" (Swidler, 1979).

"The female sex is easily seduced, weak, and without much understanding. The devil seeks to vomit out disorder through women...We wish to apply masculine reasoning and destroy the folly of these women" (Migne, 1987, Vol. 42, cols. 740).

"The sentence of God on this sex of yours lives in this age; the guilt must of necessity live too. You are the devil's gateway; you are the unsealer of that forbidden tree; you are the first deserter of the divine law; you are she who persuaded him whom the devil was not valiant enough to attack. You destroyed so easily God's image, man. On account of your desert-that is, death-even the Son of God had to die" (Quain, 1959, p. 117).

"Just as the spirit (male interior) like the masculine understanding, holds subject the appetite of the soul through which we command the members of the body, and justly imposes moderation on its helper, in the same way the man must guide the woman and not let her rule over the man; where that indeed happens, the household is miserable and perverse" (Migne, 1987, Vol. 34, col. 205).

The implications of the view that men dominate women have also been the justification for men to enforce that control. The control component of patriarchy and the assumption of ownership of women and children by men open the door to violence and abuse. The assault rate on children of parents who subscribe to the belief of male dominance is 136 percent higher than for couples not committed to male dominance (Helfer and Kempe, 1974). Battered women, too, tend to hold traditional views about sex roles in the home. Mental health workers and battered women shelter workers report that the religious beliefs of their clients seem to reinforce passivity and serve as a hindrance to effective confrontation of domestic violence and abuse (Walker, 1984). The concept of the male spiritual head even influences some religious counseling in domestic violence cases. Battered women are told to submit to their abusive husbands because the husband is the God-given headship. Since the subordination of woman to man's dominance is taught as the expression of God's intentions and not as the result of sin, female submission is viewed as a necessary requirement for getting to heaven and avoiding eternal torment.

The chronology of Eve's creation and her role in the fall is used as the foundation for the belief that women are morally inferior to men and should not trust their own judgment. Such belief favors the view that women are led into spiritual error and, for that reason, God commands her not to usurp authority over the man. Such a view reinforces the idea that women should ignore their feelings about the will of God and obey their husbands as being the representatives of God (Handford, 1972).

There is a connection between the association of femininity with defectiveness and defilement and the association of masculinity with spirituality and divinity. It is alleged that the woman is held responsible for the entry of sin into the world and for the fall of the man. Even the natural process of female menstruation, childbirth, and lactation is often viewed as offensive and evil. Because Christ and the 12 disciples were men; because the names of God connote masculinity; and because many religious groups only allow men to assume positions of leadership and authority, there evolves the connection between masculinity and divinity.

The belief that women are morally defective, unable to thrust their inner sense of what is right and wrong, and that men reflect more of the divine image than women, will render women submissive to abuse and unable to confront it. When women are taught not to trust themselves, then they relinquish their power and lose their ability to confront and resist destructive actions done against them and their children (Kroeger and Beck, 1996).

People, who are placed in positions of subordination because of religious beliefs or culture, develop certain characteristics to please people in dominance. These traits include passivity, submissiveness, dependency, lack of initiative, docility, and the inability to decide, think or act for themselves (Miller, 1986). In certain religious settings, these are the qualities that are still desirable for "good Christian women." In fact, the male-dominated model generally causes religious leaders to describe a spiritually healthy Christian woman as being submissive in the home, gentle and soft spoken, dependent, passive, non-critical, and finding identity through the husband. These same traits are not associated with the spiritually healthy male.

Women who submit to a traditional model of female subordination to men generally have a lower self-esteem than women who believe in equality and partnership between men and women (Heggen, 1989). Battered women tend to have low self-esteem (Walker, 1984). We have discovered that in more than 25 years of counseling that women remain in abusive marriages when they are taught that meekness and submissiveness should be practiced and that their resistance to violence or even reporting such violence violates biblical principles.

Some abused women believe that they are responsible for the man's behavior (Beardsley and Spry, 1975). We have encountered women who are convinced that their husband's abusive actions are the direct result of their wrong attitudes and failure to submit. They are advised to give up their power of responsibility to choose and to invest themselves in the welfare of their husbands by becoming silent. One woman revealed that she was taught that her highest moral obligation is the preservation of her marriage and the satisfaction of her husband regardless of his behavior.

The Proper Interpretation and Response

The factors that dictate religious thought regarding male-female relationship are derived from the various interpretations of the Genesis narrative, the patriarchal language of the Old Testament, the New Testament epistles, and even the writings of the Church Fathers. The implications of the mismanagement of such terms as head, covering, submission, silence, and authority have proven faulty to the point of justifiable abuse.

Abuse is an individual issue and an expression of personal choice.

However, when the recipient of abuse and the administrator of such abuse feels justified because of a misunderstanding of religious thought, then the liability shifts. This relationship between abuse and religious thought raises an issue of considerable concern for pastoral care. Pastoral attitudes about the value and the role of women must be reformed if they are contributing to such damage. If male-oriented theologies, religious beliefs, and church practices tend to foster violence against women, then a reorientation is necessary. The church has an obligation to stop abuse and to protect the victim (Matt. 18:15-17; 1 Thes. 5:14; 2 Thes. 3:15; 1 Tim. 5:20; Titus 3:2-1; Jam. 5:19-20). Furthermore, any teaching that supports the position that women are guilty, morally inferior to men, created less in the image of God, and should distrust their own judgment is a teaching in contradiction to sound biblical doctrine.

It is important to recognize that sin introduces conflict into the male-female relationship. Like divorce, this conflict is not God's original intention (Mat. 19:3-8). Toil (Gen. 3:17-19), labor pains (3:16), and death (3:19) are all results of the fall. If the fall and sin introduced a distortion of the male-female relationship (Gen. 3:6-19), then the consequence of salvation is a correction of such distortion for those who are living under God's grace through faith in Christ. (Rom. 5:12, 17-19; 1 Cor. 15:22).

Summary

*There are certain religious beliefs that justify the abuse of women.

*Extreme doctrines of male headship and female submission put an individual, family, or even a congregation at a risk of abuse.

*The Bible can be misused to hurt and reinforce destructive behavior.

*Many of the traditional religious concepts of male dominance, female submission and female inferiority correlate with some of the reasons behind abuse in the marriage and family.

*Women, at times, use the Bible to uphold or tolerate their own abuse.

*Certain biblical words or terms have been misunderstood and/ or misinterpreted to reinforce the male-dominated model.

*We must exercise spiritual intelligence in order to gain wisdom in devising church and family hierarchies. The implications of operating without it in these matters can be devastating and even dangerous.

14

THE KINGDOM OF GOD, THE BELIEVER, AND THE SUPERNATURAL

Scholars of all kinds have been on a quest for accuracy in the interpretation of historic truths, facts, and events and their consistent implementation into some practical, adaptable form. Whenever these historic truths are misunderstood or taken out of context, the consequences are confusion, skepticism, suspicion, distrust, and even disdain. However, the correction of the abuse of Biblical principles and practices is not reason for their discontinuation, debasement or disregard. A more effective strategy is a recovery of a proper understanding of the original intent and priority of such factors. A critical factor in the resolution of this matter is the Kingdom of God.

Description of the Kingdom

The Kingdom of God is the concept that defines reality, purpose and values. It is the expressed rule of God in the domain of salvation. It is both redemptive and providential. That is, it demonstrates Divine power and purpose in the salvation of the individual but also in the organization and management of all creation. The Kingdom of God is not limited to any earthly restrictions or can it be identified with any social, political, national, racial, or organization. The principles thereof define righteousness in every sphere of human existence. The discussion of any topic of theological significance cannot be separate from an understanding of the Kingdom of God. This is especially true when we explore the idea of the believer and the supernatural.

The Kingdom of God reveals the sphere of Divine government. It addresses four areas:

1) The nature and character of God. We must have a proper knowledge of the identity, authority, and ways of the Lord. We must look to the Scripture, the life and ministry of Jesus and the ongoing work of the Holy Spirit for this understanding.

2) The restoration of Divine purposes and intentions for all creation. We must have a clear understanding of what it means to occupy, take dominion, and to be fruitful and multiply.

3) Divine involvement in human affairs. There are biblical guidelines for human relationships and for all the activities, organizations, institutions, laws, and legislation that are to govern and preserve all of creation. God's involvement in human affairs is through the revelation of principles, as well as models of righteousness through the Church that can be expressed in the world.

4) The strategies for human response: God still imparts strategies for the manifestation of His will and purposes in the earth. We must know the methods by which believers can respond to Divine authority. There must be ways for the believer to respond and express these principles, precepts, and power in every sphere of human existence.

The Kingdom of God is the concept that influences the attitude and behavior of a believer. It defines values and purpose. It reveals God as the Creator, Organizers and Maintainer of all things (Gen. 1-3; 1 Chr. 29:11-12; Psalm 22:28; 24:1; 72:8; Dan. 4:7; 5:21-22; 11:34, 44, 45; Acts 17:24-31). It is past, present, and future (Rom. 14:17; 1 Cor. 15:24, 50; Gal. 5:21; Eph. 5:5; Col. 1:13; 4:11; 2 Thess. 1:5). It is neither defined nor restricted by this world nor is it an organization, institution, or something that can be constructed by humanity. The Kingdom of God in some dimension is within the believer, as the indwelling Holy Spirit (Rom. 14:17).

The Kingdom can be viewed as an alternative society (Luke 6:20); institutional church (Matt. 16:19); theocracy (Rev. 21-22); future hope (John 18:36); or present day blessing (Luke 17:20-21). Each of these concepts partially explains the perception of the rule of God, but taken individually, they fall short. A critical description of the Kingdom is the manifestation of authority or power. After delivering a demon-possessed person, Jesus said that his ability to cast out demons by the Spirit of God while on earth, meant that the Kingdom was present at that moment (Matt. 12:28; Luke 11:20). Paul writes that the Kingdom is not in word but in power (1 Cor. 4:20). Furthermore, the Kingdom of God is righteousness, peace and joy in the Holy Spirit (Rom. 14:17). An understanding of the Kingdom comes with spiritual intelligence, for it is not something that can at all be experienced or even recognized with natural intelligence.

Consequences of Varying Views

Our perceptions of the Kingdom influence our attitudes and

behaviors. For example, if the Kingdom is perceived as being something to come in the future and a reality that is heavenly and spiritual, then we will not focus on our present day stewardship to influence our culture. There will be an emphasis on prayer, inner life development, and a hope focused upon future developments. The deterioration of the environment will be viewed as the judgment of God. Believers then tend to become cultural critics, condemning and judging human failure and the dredges of sin. Indeed, they should become cultural architects who actively engage the power of the Spirit and salvation truths to effect change and influence human conditions. Such a view will restrict the supernatural to personal healings, deliverance, answer to prayer, and unusual material provisions.

If Christians view God's Kingdom only as present and material, then they will focus simply upon the symptoms of sin such as poverty, drug addiction, prejudice, and oppression. Change is then directed toward the established government, policies, laws, legislation, organizations, and institutions. As a result of a focus on earthly systems to bring solutions, the supernatural and the spiritual realm will become a fable. The believer becomes ruled by the laws of practicality, relevance, and profitability of all strategies and neglects the spiritual realm that should govern the manifestation of human ingenuity as seen in politics, education, science, commerce, communication, and entertainment.

Some Christians view the Kingdom as being focused in the institutions of churches. Such a focus moves the believers to be limited to evangelism, church growth and programs to nurture the congregations. The work of the Kingdom becomes subject to programs that entertain and maintain the congregation and potential converts. The idea of miracles, signs and wonders during the gathering of the church is minimized or can be dismissed if they could not be controlled or scheduled.

If the Kingdom is viewed as a theocracy in which God rules over all things, then we can develop a passivity that looks to God to be responsible for functions that should be under human function. A theocracy is often viewed as the reconstruction of society based upon Old Testament laws and regulation. It also mandates an intolerance for any other religions since Christianity and theocracy will be viewed as being synonymous.

If Christians view the Kingdom as a plural concept that is Divine with human involvement, then our concept of the supernatural takes on a different meaning. The supernatural becomes like "leaven" and "seeds" that are planted as ideas, concepts, principles, and strategies that influence the construction of government, laws, legislation, organizations, institutions, and the preservation of the earth with all of its rivers, streams, mountains, trees, animals, and life. The supernatural becomes a transformed life; a productive citizen; advancements in technology; communication; and cooperation between all cultural, racial, and ethnic groups. It generates a respect for all human life and a responsibility for welfare for the neighbor near and far away. It will foster proper parenting and healthy relationships. It will create a healthy respect for differences in culture and eliminate the unhealthy distinctions given to race, gender, and socioeconomic positions.

Supernatural Connection

When the identity, privileges, and responsibilities of the Kingdom of God are understood, then the connection between the believer and the supernatural is clear. The earth is to be filled with the knowledge of the glory of the Lord. Glory speaks of the visible manifestation of the invisible attributes of God. It represents God as Creator, Organizer, and Maintainer. Glory expresses the priorities, order, and purposes of Divine authority.

The supernatural is the realm of Divine authority expressed through the inadequacy of human agency. It is the establishment of laws, legislation, order, purpose, and design in every sphere of human existence. While the supernatural may be expressed as miracles, signs and wonders, it is also the reformation of thoughts, ideas, values, and objectives in government, education, science, athletics, entertainment, and commerce. The interconnection of the Kingdom of God, the believer, and the supernatural expresses something far greater than angelic visitations, prophetic utterances; visions; dreams; and signs. It is authority with design to influence the course and purpose of all creation, and that creation includes the church, home and marketplace.

Summary

*The Kingdom of God defines reality, purpose and values. It is both redemptive and providential.
*The Kingdom of God demonstrates Divine power and purpose

in the salvation of the individual but also in the organization and management of all creation.

*The supernatural is an expression of sovereignty of God and His Divine rule. It is the manifestation of the power of the Holy Spirit.

*The manifestation of the power of the Holy Spirit must not be separated from the wisdom and knowledge of the Word.

*The interconnection between the Kingdom of God, the believer, and the supernatural is expressed in power and purpose.

*One must have spiritual intelligence to recognize or begin to understand the Kingdom of God.

15

PENTECOSTAL POWER OR PSYCHIC PHENOMENON?

As aforementioned, the crisis of faith has always been conceptual. It has resided in the interpretation of Divine events and purposes and their integration into the dimensions of life. The supernatural is a ministration of the Holy Spirit and the validation of human obedience to the Divine commission (Mark 16:15-18). Spiritual intelligence is necessary for a productive interaction between the supernatural and our daily lives. This is especially true in making a distinction between the supernatural power of God and psychic phenomenon.

A number of years ago, we came across a book titled *Harper's Encyclopedia of Mystical and Paranormal Experience* by Rosemary Ellen Gulley. The book sparked our interest since the issue of Pentecostal power and the devil often surfaced in Bible studies. The Scripture reveals many individuals who bewitched or misguided the people of God through prophecy, teaching, counsel, and the display of unusual powers of divination (1 Sam. 15:15; 18:10; 19:9; 1 Chr. 21:1; Acts 8:9-11; 13:6-11; 2 C9r. 4:4; 10:4-6; Col. 2:18; 2 Pet. 3:1-4). Some of these included the witch of Endor (1 Sam. 28:7), the prophets of Baal (1 Kings 16-19), Simon the magician (Acts 8:9), Elymas the false prophet (Acts 13:8), and others.

Because the people of God were accustomed to the supernatural, it was likely that they would entertain anything or anyone that mimicked or displayed supernatural powers. Even though the Scriptures record numerous warnings against the seeking of enchanters, diviners, soothsayers, palm readers, and false prophets, there were many who sought out these avenues for information (Ex. 22:18; Deut. 18:10-12). Even the New Testament apostles provide warnings against false prophets and teachers (2 Cor. 11:13; 2 Pet. 2:1; 1 John 4:1). The epistles often cite warnings and even ways of distinguishing the truth from deception (Gal. 1:6-10; Acts 11:3-16).

How did the people of God distinguish the messengers of God from those of evil? One way to determine if a prophet was real was by seeing if the prediction came true (Duet. 18:22; 1 Sam. 3:19; Jer. 28:9; Ezek. 33:33).In additions, the Lord Jesus clearly states that a tree is known by its fruit (Matt. 7:17). A good tree bears good fruit, and a bad tree yields bad fruit. Fruit refers to the manifestation or result of activities.

Still, what are we to make of fortune tellers, Ouji boards, séances, hearing voices, moving objects, etc. How do we know that the devil is not healing, providing, or speaking? What about objects flying through a room unassisted and sounds coming from inanimate objects? These questions will be answered in general, but first, we must understand the distinctions of psychic phenomena.

Key Terms

First of all, what is psychic phenomenon? Is it evil or extraordinary human ability? What are some of the common examples of this activity? Perhaps a few definitions are necessary. Consider the following:

Orthodoxy - ideas or beliefs generally accepted as the norm.

Heresy - beliefs and behaviors that contradict the norm.

Supernatural - divine activity that transcends human capability

Miracles - expression of sovereignty of God over times, circumstances and people.

Psychic phenomena - display of human or demonic power

Spiritualism - a religious movement that began in 1848 that purported evidence of survival after death, manifested through mediums who communicated with spirits and performed paranormal feats.

Clairaudience - the hearing of sounds, music, and voices not audible to normal hearing. It is often experienced in a dream state and related to stages of consciousness. A clairvoyant dream may feature a message whispered by an unknown voice. The voices have been perceived as those of angels, God, spirits of the dead, spirit guides, and the formless Divine Force.

Clairvoyance - the perception of current objects, events, or people that may not be discerned through the normal senses. The seeing may manifest in internal or external visions, or a sensing of images. Clairvoyance overlaps with other psychic faculties and phenomena, such as clairaudience, clairsentience, telepathy, recognition, retro-cognition, psychometry, and remote viewing.

Glossolalia - the act of speaking or writing in another unknown tongue. It denotes the baptism of the Holy Spirit in Pentecostal or charismatic Christian worship. Some of the tongues are intelligible and some are not.

Fortean phenomena - any paranormal phenomena that defies natural explanation, such as a rain of frogs, fish, stones, dead birds, flies, and snakes; mystifying religious experiences, such as stigmata, the sudden flowing of blood from a person's palm or legs; weeping statues; spontaneous human combustion; ghosts and etc.

Psychometry - a psychic skill in which information about people, places, and events is obtained by the handling of objects associated with them. Information is received through clairvoyance, telepathy, retro-cognition, and precognition.

Séance - event in which a medium contacts the spirit world. The medium enters an altered state of consciousness and reaches a spirit, called a control or "spirit friend" or "spirit helper." The control communicates mentally with the medium by speaking directly through his or her vocal cords, conveying information from other spirits

Psychic attack - a paranormal attack upon humans or animals that causes physical or mental distress, injury, illness, or even death. This can be the equivalent of a curse. The most common symptoms of psychic attack is the "hag syndrome" in which the victim is awakened feeling a crushing weight on the chest accompanied by paralysis. In some instances, the victim may see a form, hear a noise, or smell vile odors. Nightmares occur in some cases. Other symptoms include feelings of overwhelming dread and fear, which deteriorate to nervous exhaustion, mental breakdown, a physical wasting of the body, an invisible presence evoking a feeling of horror, a sensation of pressure on the chest, and tearing pain.

Magic - the ability to affect change in accordance through the will of a magician or the supernatural.

Near-death Experiences (NDE) - a sense of being dead, or an out-of-body experience in which one feels floating above the body, looking down; cessation of pain and a feeling of bliss or peacefulness; travelling down a dark tunnel toward a light at the end; meeting nonphysical beings who glow, many of whom are dead friends and relatives; coming in contact with a guide or Supreme Being who takes them on a life review, during which their entire life is put into perspective without remembering any negative judgment about past acts, and a reluctant return to life.

Teleportation - the movement of bodies or objects over

great distances; a form of psychokinesis.

Psychokinesis - the influence of mind over matter through invisible means, such as the movement of objects, bending metals, and the outcome of events. Magic, spells, curses, and rituals to control the weather may involve this.

Theosophy - a philosophical system that claims that knowledge or a transcendent reality can be gained through revelation or the practice of the occult tradition. The Greek word, "theosophy" is a combination of the words theos, "god," and sophia, "wisdom." Theosophy claims that all religions stem from the same root of ancient wisdom.

Prophecy - a divinely inspired vision or revelation of people, circumstances, nations, countries, or even great events to come. All prophecies come from precognition or knowledge of the future, but not all precognitive experiences are prophecies. The key difference is the source and intention.

Precognition - the direct knowledge or perception of the future, obtained through extraordinary means (ESP). It occurs through dreams, waking visions, auditory hallucinations, thoughts that flash into the mind, and a sense of "knowing." Precognitive knowledge may be induced through trance, channeling, mediumship, and divination.

Mainstream vs. Alternative Religious Movements

In our contemporary world, there are mainstream and alternative religious movements. Social scientists divide alternative religious movements into three groups: churches, sects, and cults. Churches are large denominations that fit within the prevailing culture; sects are groups that have broken away from denominations, such as Quakers, Jehovah's Witness, etc.; and cults are groups that follow structures alien to the prevailing environment. The term "cult" is subject to definition. For example, in our Western society, Hinduism and Buddhism are cults while Christianity is a cult in the East. It is common for the prevailing religion to denounce other groups.

Alternative religious movements appeal to people in all socioeconomic groups. Like alternative medicine, their appeal rests somewhat in their similarity and dissimilarity to the prevailing religious communities. Their memberships are not restricted to the "fringes of society" of people who reside outside the "norms" of the culture. To the contrary, these movements attract the educated, wealthy, single, young, upper middle class, and urban adults. In our contemporary culture, alternative religious groups offer a diet of social, spiritual, and psychological support that is attractive to some aspects of the society. Competition exists between mainline churches and these marginal religious groups mainly because of the principle of supply and demand. In a culture that is dominated by the desire for wealth, health, and long life, alternative groups seek to fill these needs. At times the distinction between alternative and mainline groups is so blurred that they find themselves ministering to the same congregations. In fact, some seekers find it comfortable and edifying to attend both groups.

What then is the dividing line between these Christian and non-Christian communities and between the psychic and Pentecostal power? Is it the centrality of Jesus Christ, the Bible, water baptism, altar calls, or gospel preaching? It would be easy to say that Jesus Christ and the gospel are the dividing lines. However, even among mainline Christian groups, there are allegations that there is "another Jesus" and "another gospel" being preached. In our contemporary society, Christian movements are critiqued and examined for their "orthodoxy" or their departure from the faith. So some distinctions are made regarding the source, intent, and nature of the doctrine and practice of the manifestations.

Divine or Demonic

A classic distinction between Pentecostal power and psychic phenomena rests in the purpose or intention of an action, or manifestation. Let us consider some basic characteristics of demonic influences as opposed to divine influences.

The first consideration is the relationship of the action to traditional religious standards. When a course of action departs from traditional patterns and is unable to reconcile such differences, there is a danger that evil may be operating. However, it must be remembered that all reformation movements and most of the principles and practices that accompany them are in defiance of existing "orthodox" religious standards. In essence, change has always been a deviation from the norm.

The second concern is whether the action breeds liberty, love, and harmony or schism and hate. The wisdom that proceeds from above is peaceful, without partiality and easy to entreat. When the Spirit of the Lord is at work, there is liberty, love, and the fostering of interpersonal relationships. Those who claim inspiration and preach hate, judgment, and division should question the source of their message. Furthermore, when there is excessive authoritarianism and domination, there is a stifling of creativity and fostering of immaturity. Growth and maturity occur when people are taught to make their own decisions and assume responsibility for them.

The third concern is change and expansion. Divine inspiration and guidance produces fruits of creativity, growth, development, increased consciousness, and awareness. Whenever fear, antagonism, criticism, condemnation, and guilt are used to dull the conscience of people to the world beyond themselves and limit their participation with people of other groups, cultures, races, and nations, then the spiritual motivation and source should be highly suspect. The demonic narrows the consciousness of life beyond the local group and stifles creativity and innovation. Stagnation or even regression is usually the result.

A fourth fruit of the demonic is the absence of joy and peace. Whenever people are constantly criticized, accused, and dominated, there is creation of spiritual and emotional anguish. The Holy Spirit stimulates freedom, open, and honest exchange between people. Domination always hinders the exchange of honest communication. Such manipulation and domination can ultimately destroy the personal identity of any individual, and its source is likely demonic.

Baptism in the Holy Spirit is not a Pentecostal or Charismatic phenomenon, but rather it is a norm of the Christian experience. Every believer receives the Holy Spirit. As aforementioned, the Holy Spirit is the mediator of all heavenly-earthly transactions. In addition to all of the work of the Holy Spirit, the baptism in the Spirit provides spiritual gifts to believers and enables them to pray in a spirit-directed language called tongues (Acts 10:44-47; 19:1-6; 1 Cor. 12:28-30). Unfortunately, most Spirit-baptized believers use less than 10 percent of the purposes and benefits of speaking in tongues (1 Cor. 12:28-30). There is Biblical proof and many personal benefits for speaking in these "unknown tongues." Dr. Bill Hamon in his book"70 Reasons for Speaking in Tongues," reveals some most significant reasons for speaking in "the tongues of men and of angels" (1 Cor. 13:1). He includes prayer, activation of gifts and fruits, discernment, edification, communion, rest, and many other personal benefits.

When we pray in tongues, our language originates from our inner spirit and not from the natural mind. It is not a learned language, but a gift from the Holy Spirit. For that reason, the natural mind does not comprehend its meaning (1 Cor. 14:14).

Speaking in tongues should not be associated with demonic power. To determine if an action is divine or demonic, we must look at what the act or encounter produced. In other words, what type of fruit does it yield? Does it stimulate growth and maturity or stifle growth and foster immaturity? Does it generate a consciousness of God or does it popularize the miracle worker? In all of the miracles performed by the Lord Jesus and even the apostles, all of the recipients were liberated. They became disciples but not addicts. Above all, the conscience of the people was elevated, causing them to worship God. They became aware that the love of God transcended their cultural and social consciousness. The fruit is always good when God is involved.

Summary

*There is a distinction between work of the Holy Spirit and other supernatural forces.

*The distinction between the true and the false rests in the source and intent of the manifestation.

*The fruit or outcome of a manifestation will help determine its source. Good fruit can only come from a good tree and bad fruit from a bad tree.

*The Holy Spirit generates liberty, love, harmony, and not schism nor hatred.

*The demonic narrows the consciousness of life beyond the local group; stifles creativity and innovation; and depreciates joy and peace.

16

THEOLOGY OF ASSOCIATION

C hristianity is not an incentive-driven faith. Although it provides tremendous benefits and privileges in this life and the one to come, the gospel message is not sprinkled with offers of gifts for repentance. Materialism is not the central focus of faith. In fact, the focus of one's faith is an indication of its character. Admittedly, an enthusiastic preacher can make offers and declarations that border on incentives. Hence, the nature of conversion is a matter of personal faith based on the content of the message preached and believed. For this reason, there are descriptors such as "feigned faith," "unfeigned faith," "shipwreck faith" and even presumption. When beliefs and expectations are either contradicted or not realized, then the character of faith is revealed. For what reason did one believe? For what reason was there identification with Jesus in water baptism and public confession of belief? Was it to escape a fiery reservation; to reach a place of eternal bliss; to prosper in earthly things; or to be happy and content in this present life? The motive for salvation determines the character of faith.

The character of faith is expressed in several narratives. In Samaria, Philip preaches Jesus and Kingdom of God, and the people believe (Acts 8:5-13). When Simon the magician sees the demonstration of the Holy Spirit through Philip, he desires to purchase the power for personal gain. Peter rebukes his presumption, however, and tells him to repent (Acts 8:18-24). When the rich young ruler learns that eternal life demands loss of his possessions and becoming a disciple, he walks away. Similarly, Jesus cites the enthusiasm of the crowds that follow him are incentive driven (John 6:26-27).

The relationship between faith and motive is further expressed in our contemporary society. Oftentimes, networks, coalitions, and organizations are developed around common needs or objectives. In fact, the needs and objectives can be so compelling that even factions and antagonistic groups will form within a larger organization. However, when the motive for association is personal benefits only, the relationships will surely perish as the benefits decline.

The character of faith is dependent upon the motive for belief, so then is the quality of relationships dependent upon the motive. Human needs for assurance, acceptance, provision, safety, and even liberty will precipitate associations even across racial, ethnic, and socioeconomic boundaries. However, the association becomes a liability when anything threatens to compromise the incentives.

There are times when certain relationships become a liability. In fact, Israel was warned of the prophets not to take on the ways of surrounding nations. Yet, they were a priestly nation called to declare and demonstrate the government of God in the earth. How can they influence other nations if they were to remain separate from them? There is a distinction between "association" and "identification." Association means interaction while identification means compromise. We shall examine the idea of being involved while maintaining the distinction of our character and mission.

Historical Examples

Historically, the stringent demands and even penalties of the Law preserved Israel as a people. If they obeyed the commandments of the Lord, they would have been a priestly nation. The Law also determined the boundaries of their relationship with other nations. The prophets admonished them to be separate from other nations (Exod. 19:4-6; Deut. 14:1-2; Ezra 10:11; 1 Kings 8:53). The idea that association and identification are synonymous is also expressed in the admonitions of Proverbs 22:24 to not make friends with an angry man unless you become partaker of his character. Paul warned the Corinthians to have no company with a brother who is an adulterer, fornicator or idolater (1 Cor. 5:9). These narratives suggest the danger inherent in certain alliances. In essence, there is the risk that association with certain individuals or groups suggests an agreement with their character and beliefs.

These issues of association and disassociation seen in religious communities are also common in our contemporary society. For example, social relationships that are based upon honesty, integrity, and trust can be compromised when one of the member experiences an ethical or moral fault. Such relationships can be challenged when they are based upon similarity of beliefs and convictions. At times, organizations will excommunicate a member because of a violation of established and accepted patterns of beliefs and behavior. This is especially true in religious communities where boundaries are established by doctrines.

This principle of separation is often seen in other social relationships. For example, individuals who themselves put others at risk because of their behavior or health are sometimes isolated from the general populace. In Biblical days, the lepers were separated from the communities because their disease was contagious. Today, people who are mentally ill may be institutionalized.

The John Principle

The gospel of John records Jesus' prayer for the disciples and those who will believe on Him (John 17:1-28).

> *I pray for them, I do not pray for the world, but for those whom You have given, for they are Yours... Now I am no longer in the world, but these are in* the world, *and I come to You. Holy Father keep through You r name those You have given Me that they may be one as We are...I have given them Your word and the world has hated them because they are* not of the world, *just as I am not the world. I do not pray that You should take them* out of the world, *but that You should keep them from the evil one. They are not of the world, just as I am not of the world...As You sent Me*

into the world, I also have sent them into the
world (17:9,11, 14-16,18).

In this prayer, there are specific words that define a redemptive
attitude and relationship with the world in its lost state. Notice
these phrases:

> "in the world" - physically
> "not of the world" - doctrinally
> "out of the world" - experientially
> "into the world" – missionally

This prayer that the disciples not be taken from the world but kept
from the evil one is most significant. It defines association without
separation. The proximity of the disciples to people of different
thought, value, objectives, and behaviors does not endanger their
beliefs, attitudes or behavior, for their redemptive experience and
empowerment transformed them into agents of influence. In
our contemporary world, this prayer is a commission for us to be
involved with others for the sake of influence. Like the disciples,
we are kept from the evil through discernment, which enables us
to distinguish that which is right from that which is wrong.

Association and Identification

In an international gathering of leaders, the comment was made
that two cannot walk together unless they agree (Amos 3:3). Most
everyone in the group agreed except me. I responded stating
that Amos posed a question that the Lord had already answered.
The Lord had walked with Israel for years and had never agreed

with them. There was laughter among the entire group, but then questions began to arise. How can we work with other ministries if we have significant differences of thought and belief? The comment was the catalyst for a discussion that lasted for almost an hour. This latter statement has served as justification for many ministry relationships to remain distant or separate. When beliefs and practices conflict, then disassociation has often occurred.

Amos 3:3 is often misunderstood or misinterpreted. Indeed, there are times when disassociation is necessary. In fact, there may be a need to re-evaluate the motives for our association. If personal gain and profitability are the only motives, then the dissolution of some partnerships and relationships are justifiable when they are no longer beneficial.

The admonition to be separate and distinct must be kept in context with the commission to go into all the world and make disciples of nations (Mark 16:15). There can be association without the compromise of beliefs and convictions. In essence, association does not always mean identification. Two can walk together and not agree when the reason for the association is clear. Oneness does not mean sameness. Light shines into darkness. Influence is still a virtue. The integrity of relationships and friendships should not be so easily broken because of differences of opinions. Before the formation or dissolution of a relationship, association, or partnership, the motive needs to be evaluated.

We must see ourselves as redemptive agents. Therefore, our

assignment as disciples, preachers, teachers and so forth has nothing to do with our feelings. Like Jonah, we can't get caught up in what we feel or think about the people to whom we are assigned. Our mission, like Christ, is to finish the mission or assignment. As such, we must subject our emotions and ideas to Biblical principles, not world standards. This will require spiritual intelligence rather than human wisdom.

Summary

* What you seek to receive from God determines the nature of your faith.

*Staying away from certain people with undesirable or dissimilar practices has historically been practiced both in religious and secular communities.

*Association and identification are different. We can associate with people and not identify with their lifestyle such that it compromises our principles.

*We must examine why we associate with an individual or group as a basis to determine if we are on a mission from God or for our own benefit.

*We will need spiritual intelligence to form Christ-principled associations.

17

SPIRITUAL MOMENTUM

Intelligence is acquired knowledge. It is conceptual and relates to ideas, concepts, and convictions. It is for this reason that processes and experiences are indispensable for wisdom and understanding. Life is filled with experiences, opportunities and choices even though we do not always have control of them. If we were infallible creatures with absolute foresight, then we could predict the outcome of all decisions. However, our humanity has not given us such a privilege. As a result, we encounter events, circumstances, and even people that hinder our progress. While these may be catalogued as social, economic and even spiritual, we do have the option of going on, standing still, or simply falling away.

Our faith, expressed in one form via spiritual intelligence, is progressive and growing. In other words, it has momentum; it should be dynamic, not stagnant. From the creation narrative recorded in the book of Genesis to the consummation of all things that are witnessed in Revelation, there is gradual unfolding of knowledge, truth, experiences, and events. While Genesis is a seed bed of revelation truth in which concepts, principles, and practices are introduced, there is a gradual movement from types, symbols, and metaphors to realities. From one blood to many nations and from a few disciples to a global network of believers, there is a progression from the one to the many and from the simple to the complex. Yet within this faith economy, there is the timeless and timely, lesser and greater. That is, there are significant and insignificant matters which should engage our time and attention appropriately. Additionally, some beliefs and practices continue or never change despite the evolution of new generations of humanity (timeless) while the strategies and methods of implementation evolve and adapt to address new times and seasons (timely).

Each generation should comprehend the many promises, privileges, and responsibilities for those who believe. The new birth offers forgiveness of sins; deliverance from the power of evil; baptism in the Holy Spirit; the dynamics of faith and hope; privilege of prayer; access to Divine things; ability to comprehend spiritual truths; and the right to eternal life. Yet, as previously mentioned, Christianity is not an incentive-driven faith. Despite its promises and privileges, these incentives must be understood as motives for responsibilities as opposed to some kind of payment or affirmation that God is paying attention. For example, in the book of Job, Satan suggests that Job only serves God because of incentives, and if those incentives were taken away, then Job would turn from God. However, Job lost everything and remained true and firm in his faith. If salvation is viewed only as a doorway to earthly pleasures and benefits, then the absence of such provisions can potentially create a crisis of faith. This is a critical distinction, for when it is not understood, many believers fall away from the faith. John asserted that those who leave the faith, were never actually true believers. He said, "They went out from us, but they did not really belong to us; for if they had been of us, they would have continued with us; but they went out that they might be made manifest, that none of them were of us." (1 John 2:19).

Progressive Faith

It must be understood that the existence of challenges, difficulties, deficiencies, and even persecutions may be consequence of living in a world organized on wrong principles (1 John 2:15-17). It is interesting that Paul writes to the Philippians that he has learned to be content in whatever state he experiences; he can be abased or abound (Phil. 4). In fact, Paul encourages the youthful Timothy to endure hardness as a good soldier and not be entangled with the affairs of this life (2 Tim. 2:1-4). Such life experiences do not occur simply because of a lack of faith; ignorance of the promises of God; and rebellion or sin. It is somewhat presumptuous to believe that every problem experienced in life is due to a spiritual deficiency, a human failure, or even a Divine test to prove faith. This non-utopian world offers its share of challenges regardless of the spiritual status of the believer. Still, we always have the promise and privilege of deliverance. If there are no challenges in our faith equation, then all the blessings of God are defined as simply tangible earthly things. That is, when these "blessings" are not always evident in material provisions, then it is possible for faith to become shipwrecked.

The progress of faith rests in maintaining a right relationship between promise, privilege, responsibility, and challenge. Whether in abundance or scarcity, contentment must be learned in all circumstances of life. Our love for God is not simply because of earthly pleasures He provides, but because we have been given the right to participate in a tremendous mission. That mission is to be an example of the believer in word, in conversation, in charity, in spirit, in faith, and in purity (1 Tim. 4:12).

As aforementioned, Christianity is progressive and the admonition to grow in grace and in the knowledge of the Lord rests in the willingness to embrace and implement truth. Our world increases or shrinks according to people and ideas we include or exclude. Nature reveals the idea of birth and growth. Each spring, I witness the birth and progressive development of birds and ducklings. Their existence is dependent upon the ability and willingness to learn survival skills in a timely manner. They must conform to a pattern within a particular cycle of time. Failure to do so is not a viable alternative. They cannot contend with the survival skills of their predecessors/parent. No generation gap or old school versus new school concept exists. The wisdom and instincts of the generation sustains them.

Like our faith, human existence is a growing, progressive cycle of experiences. That cycle can be continuous or interrupted. The interruption can be due to a variety of factors, such as health, relationships, education, occupation, or economic issues.

It is possible to become distracted along the journey and make decisions with some very negative lifelong consequences. The willingness to recover from difficulties and continue the journey is the key to successful living. The choices to quit, recover or continue are options available to everyone. In other words, failure is only possible if we quit.

The biblical records countless examples of stagnation, regression, and even resistance to change among those in the faith community. This sustained immaturity is experienced conceptually and behaviorally. For example, a whole nation of people can experience God, His purposes and His power but are seemingly unable to grasp this principle of progressive revelation and the unfolding of truth. The epistle to the Hebrews reveals a classic assessment of this sustained immaturity, stating that when Israel should be teachers, they still have need of someone to teach them (Heb. 5:12). The Galatians epistle rebukes a people who are unwilling to relinquish their slavish obedience to the law for a wonderful revelation of grace through faith in Christ Jesus (3:1-29). Paul's letter to the Romans begins with an analysis of a historical crisis involving a people who knew God but did not retain the knowledge of God in their consciousness (1:20-32). In fact, they changed the image of the living God into things made with their hands and even worshipped the images and even the human creatures. Paul, himself, reveals his own journey from immaturity to maturity in a letter to the Corinthians where he cites the difference between the spiritual man and the natural man (1 Cor. 2:6-16). Paul even cites his progression in thought for when he was a child, he thought and acted as one, but maturity did come (1 Cor. 13:11). These examples reveal a progression and growing of faith in which individuals were either willing or unwilling to progress and expand their borders of experience, knowledge and behavior.

To fully understand the progression of faith, we must understand that our world expands or diminishes according to the ideas, beliefs, and people we include or exclude. If we reject the unknown and unfamiliar without a proper consideration of its value, then the circumference of our world remains constant. If we choose to consider that there is value in new ideas, different experiences, and other people, then we become candidates for admission into a larger worldview. Consider some historical records of shifts in technology. The people who experience the horse and buggy were not initially as trusting of the new "gasoline carriage." They were quite familiar with the requirements and demands of the horse and buggy but the new horseless buggy was not as predictable or familiar. Furthermore, the idea of air travel and other technological advancements has always been met with skepticism, doubt, and even opposition.

Challenges to Change

Skepticism and reluctance are not always a resistance to change, but may at times, represent a desire for clarity and assurance. The farmer and the traveler may desire a more efficient and faster product, but they desire to know if the alternative will be beneficial. The same can be said of our faith and how new ideas and understanding affect us. A desire for clarity can at times be misinterpreted as a resistance to change or progress. For example, long standing patterns of thought and behavior have emotional components. These emotional components generate a dependency, reliance, and a comfort level with that which is familiar and trustworthy. The problem is that "familiarity breeds contempt" for change. Consequently, during times of transition and the introduction of new ideas and patterns of thought, information and dialogue are indispensable. Moments of discovery should cause discussions over the issues and areas of concern about the old and the new. As a result, fundamental questions will need to be addressed. What is wrong with the old? Why is there a need for a change? Is the new alternative dependable? Will there be loses? Will there be major disruptions in the status quo of relationships, structure, goals, and values? These are viable questions that must be addressed for the growth to be true and sustainable.

As aforementioned, traditions have a strong emotional component because of their longevity, familiarity, popularity, and dependability. Longstanding patterns of thought, attitude, and behavior are guarded because they have emotional acquaintances. Consequently, any disruption or effort to replace these psychological and behavioral friends is met with resistance. However, if new alternatives can be introduced as supplements and shown to be beneficial, the transition can be acceptable and successful.

Generally, when changes are made, a crisis in the transition usually occurs and is the result of an unfortunate mistake. It is the tendency to depreciate the present or status quo in order to validate the new alternative. For some people, in order to give credibility to a new pattern of thought, attitude, and behavior, they feel a need to expose and magnify the deficiencies and inadequacies in the old one. Hence, they believe credibility (of the new) demands discredit (of the old). This effort to devalue, denounce, and even destroy popular traditions often meets opposition. A more productive strategy would be to embrace traditions for their contribution and introduce the alternative not as an enemy but as a friend. This is most effectively done when an atmosphere of conciliation, not antagonism, is created.

Growth and opportunity expand whenever memory and imagination are merged. Whenever the present culture of beliefs, convictions, values, and priorities opens the door to new residents of people and ideas, then opportunities are limitless. Stagnation in reference to faith is not always the products of ignorance, but rather it can be symptoms of fear of uncertainty and an unwillingness or stubbornness to change because of a lack of clarity. Change demands answers to critical questions. What is wrong with the old? Why do we need something different? What will we do with the old? Have we been wrong? Appropriate and affable answers to such questions create an atmosphere of trust. This is especially true when there is a genuine respect for the contribution of the old and a pattern is established for progressive thinking.

People who actively engage change and growth in their faith and its many expressions, must understand that others' desire for clarity and assurance is not necessarily a resistance to change. That is, longstanding patterns of thought and behavior generated an emotional dependency because they are familiar and predictable. New thoughts and ideas have not yet been tested for their dependability. Hence, it is not uncommon for there to exist a need for assurance that the new will be profitable and beneficial and not destructive. To return to a previous metaphor, a demand for understanding of how the "gasoline horse" is to be integrated into the economy of the horse and buggy requires some persuasion. Reformation requires information, conversation, and clarification.

Our initial premise is the idea of momentum and growth and reasons for stagnation and immaturity. What stimulates growth and advancement and what stops the process? Nature reveals that the fledgling bird must be pushed out of the nest to learn to fly. The lioness ceases to nurse her cubs and they must adapt to hunting. The human growth cycle is probably not as drastic but there are moments of separation and self-discovery. The first walking step or haircut or even the initial swim in water are new experiences for the child. Even in adulthood, there can be moments of crisis where fear, anxiety, uncertainty, and skepticism develop. The loss of a relationship or a critical mistake in judgment that develops into a failed experience can stifle the growth cycle. The critical question is why? What contributes to this stagnation and loss of mobility? It can be conceptual, spiritual, or psychological. It can be wrong thinking and improper conclusions. In some ways, it is some unseen evil force that creates emotional pain and fear. Or, it is simply character flaws or personality dynamics that create addictive behavioral patterns that restrict development.

There are events and experiences in our lives that can stifle our spiritual and natural development. As aforementioned, a crisis, such as the sudden loss of a relative; the unexpected loss of a career; and even an unwanted sickness or disease, can greatly challenge psychological, behavioral, and spiritual growth. All of these negative experiences and many others can potentially shut us down, limit our movement, and imprison us in a time and space of life.

So what does it take to get us going again? If it takes a crisis to shut us down, does it take a crisis of a different nature to start us up again? After many years in ministry as a pastor and bishop of churches and as a practicing dentist, I have witnessed both natural and spiritual issues and how they affect people. I have counseled and consoled individuals from various racial, gender, ethnic, cultural, and economic backgrounds. Despite their differences, their perception of their world and their own willingness to receive and act upon ideas and alternative information have all contributed to their transformation. Those who were willing to listen and entertain the possibility that there is a future and an existence for them beyond their present status, were the ones to successfully navigate through their crisis state.

Convictions to be Changed

For momentum to occur, there are some beliefs and convictions that must be dismissed as incorrect. These include the following:

*Life consists of merely what we see
*Faith is a denial of reality

*The past is a prison

*Failure is written in ink (final)

*Age is absolute

*Kindness is weakness

*Patience is denial

*Thinking the best of others is gullibility

*First impressions are always correct

*Sickness, disease, poverty, and distress are Divine tests

*Every negative circumstance is a spiritual battleground

*Human deficiency is always a lack of faith, ignorance of promises, or rebellion

*Spiritual warfare is engaging evil

*God cannot change history

*God must be persuaded by sacrifices of prayer, offerings, etc.

*Blessings consist of an abundance of things

*Contentment can be purchased, married, divorced, or abandoned

*Verbal confession alone will correct what behavior has created

*Women are in subjection to men

*Curses are a reality for believers

*Prayer is warfare

Things Acquired and Inherited

For momentum to occur, it is important to determine what characteristics are given at birth and which ones are developed over time. My wife and I have watched the movie of Tarzan the Ape Man many times. Over the years, there have been different renditions of this epic drama that demonstrate how environmental conditioning influences human identity and behavior. As a baby,

Tarzan was raised by gorillas and chimpanzees and took on their behavioral characteristics. In fact, over time, this baby, without any human contact, assumed the identical mannerisms, language, thought, and behavior of his adopted parents, the apes. The baby grew up to be a man who looked human but acted and thought like his adopted parents. The movie demonstrates that attitudes, values, objectives, and behavior are acquired traits.

How much of Tarzan's personality was acquired at birth and how much was transmitted from the culture? Certainly, his aggression and outlook were a matter of cultural conditioning, not genetic endowments. In the movie, he appeared to be an optimist and a problem-solver, or solution-oriented individual. This was perhaps learned behavior and not capabilities acquired from birth.

When considering concepts of learned behavior versus genetically inherited behavior, it is good to also consider free will. Human free will is the God-given ability in every human being to be able to make decisions. How much of the human personality and character are a matter of self-development, though? Human development is similar to that in the animal kingdom in the sense that birth parents nurture, train, and influence their offspring. Parents teach or model things such as hygiene skills, food preparation, dietary choices, interpersonal communication, and responses to the changes and challenges of the external environment. However, there comes a time in life when individuals assume absolute control over their emotions, attitudes, beliefs, ideas, and behavior. The process is called maturation when a child becomes an adult and exercises his/her will freely without parental input or boundaries. Once people mature or become independent, their personal preferences and choices may transcend family traditions and customs.

As aforementioned, it is important to determine what behavioral characteristics are inherited at birth or developed through experiences. For years, I considered myself to be a procrastinator. "Why do today what you can do tomorrow?" I thought. So I was constantly battling with emotions of guilt and condemnation whenever opportunities were missed because the decision to act was not on time. Then I discovered that my reason for procrastinating was due to my view of the task itself. If I perceived that task to be distasteful, extremely difficult, and risky, I would delay my response or avoid it altogether. The more this strategy was used, the more it became a habit. Then I read a book by Martin Seligman titled "Learned Optimism." The author's premise was simply that optimism and pessimism are both learned behaviors. The way an individual explains an event will determine the response. Dr. Seligman calls this the *Explanatory Style* (1991). The parameters for explanation include duration (temporary or permanent), effect (specific or general), and cause (personal or environmental). When the duration, cause, and effect of any circumstance is properly explained, there is motivation for engagement. From this, I developed a catalogue of personality dynamics. It consisted of the following descriptors:

Castrophizer – considers everything as a problem
Denialist – refuses to recognize reality

Minimizer – fails to consider all factors

Idealist – waits for the perfect moment

Realist – demands proof

Procrastinator – puts off

Turtle – excludes the world of reality

Rabbit – reacts rather than acts

Lion – roars to dominate rather than solve

Bird – flies away from any distress

These personality dynamics are not exhaustive, but they express tendencies that can be changed and even dismissed. Human response to the external environment is always learned or acquired behavior. Thus, we should not automatically think that we cannot change.

As mentioned previously, certain characteristics in our lives are beyond our determination. For example, we do not have control over the time and place of our birth; the parents who conceived us; or our race, gender, or physical features. In fact, the early phase of our development renders us susceptible to the thoughts, ideas, and opinions of those who nurture us, such as parents, school teachers, and others. Still, we do have choices. In fact, as adults we have absolute control over our thoughts, ideas, beliefs, attitudes, and behaviors. Information liberates us and provides us with alternatives for choices.

Things Learned

Spiritual influences manifest themselves in practical ways, such as discernment. Confidence, uncertainty, clarity, and confusion are often emotional issues that express themselves in our behavior. Emotional components find their origin in ideas and convictions that we embrace as truth. Redemptive truth finds its source in the Scripture. Consider some of these ideas and convictions that find their origin in redemptive truth:

*Ideas and beliefs influence our attitude and behavior.

*We have absolute control over beliefs, ideas, attitudes, and behavior.

*Our world increases or decreases according to the people and ideas we include or exclude.

*If history becomes a teacher, then the future will be a friend.

*Memory and imagination must both occupy our mind.

*Two can walk together and not agree.

*Association does not always indicate identification (birds of a feather do not always flock together, and a book is not always known by its cover).

*Love never fails.

*The power of love is forgiveness.

*Forgiveness is the victory.

*Forgiveness is not memory loss, but it is memory without vengeance.

*Courage and confidence are by-products of revelation.

*Emotional pain is weakness leaving.

*Contentment must be learned.

*Happiness is a choice.

*Life is too short to be unhappy.

*The stronger always reaches out to the weaker.

*Faith works by doubt, memory, explanation, anticipation, testimony, and obedience.

*Belief requires some disbelief.

*Faith looks beyond the obvious.

*Faith is not denial of reality but the recognition of finality.

*The strength of faith is patience.

*Greed consumes and benevolence builds.

*Jealousy distracts and trust focuses.

*Prejudice blinds and fairness enlightens.

*Indifference isolates and sensitivity enlarges.

*Pride deludes and humility clarifies.

*Fear torments and confidence blesses.

*Anger imprisons and peace liberates.

*Unforgiveness grieves and forgiveness comforts.

*Selfishness diminishes while benevolence enlarges.

*Patience is a good friend to frustration.

*Unforgiveness grieves while forgiveness comforts.

*Self-doubt is unprofitable.

*Self-discovery reveals what external opinions cannot.

*Credibility of one idea does not depend upon dis-credibility of another.

*Without trust, there is no honesty.

*Anointing and gifting will open doors that only integrity will keep open.

*His will never carries you where His grace will not keep you.

*All things have a beginning and an end.

*Divine strength is made perfect in human weakness.

*Divine sufficiency is greater than all human deficiency.

*Internal unrest can be a symptom of Divine-human will conflict.

*Peace is not an absence of conflict but the privilege of knowing.

*New ideas need not always replace old ideas.

*The new and the old can work together.

*Failure is not always final unless there is quitting.

*Emotional stress can increase emotional strength.

*Emotional pain may be the departure of emotional weakness.

*Unjust criticism may represent envy and jealousy.

*Life does not consist totally in what is seen.

*History need not be a prison if we make it a teacher.

*The perceptions of the past can be changed.

*Challenges are not always avoidable but anticipation is a good ally.

*God is for us.

*Our confidence is in God.

*All things are possible with God.

*Life does not consist in the abundance of things.

*We can forgive, forget, and recover our peace, confidence, and courage.

*Change is indispensable for growth.

*We are of God.

All of these are critical assumptions that have been proven to be realities in life.

The Laws of Spiritual Momentum

Momentum is progression and growth. It is spiritual, emotional, and behavioral. It is spiritual, for it involves our convictions and beliefs. It is emotional, for it is expressed in our attitudes. It is behavioral since it is expressed in our responses and reactions to people, ideas, circumstances, and events. The aforementioned critical assumptions can be summarized into several laws that promote spiritual momentum:

Law of Self-Control

The subjection of the human will to the Word and Spirit of God is the essence of faith, hope, and obedience, that is, the willingness to respond to the command of principles rather than the demand of emotions. Emotions are wonderful friends, but they are not always dependable rulers. Consequently, reaction, which is emotion-driven, represents the power of the external environment over our behavior. Response, which is principle-driven, represents an inner supervision over the external environment.

Law of Conviction

As aforementioned, commitment to principle is commitment to predictable behavior. The relationship between belief and behavior is quite well established. It is a well-tested proposition that both individual and corporate decisions, attitudes, values, and judgments hinge upon some form of a belief system. One's belief system is usually the product of knowledge and wisdom gained through experiences and relationships in the natural and spiritual environments. Moments of discovery occur when the spiritual world of dreams, intuitions, and prophecies, reveal insight, knowledge, wisdom and understanding. When the source and content of such information is accepted as truth, then attitudes and behaviors will follow. Popularity is not always correct criteria for truth. In other words, a lot of people can be wrong.

Law of Memory

The willingness to recall significant and instructive moments and ideas is vital to mental, physical, spiritual health and momentum. Memory is creative and selective recall. While there are some memories that should be forgotten, there are some experiences that should not be forgotten. Dreams, visions, and aspirations should always be merged with the wisdom, knowledge, and understanding that comes from historic moments.

Law of Imagination

Faith looks beyond the obvious. For the joy that was set before him, the Lord Jesus suffered persecution and crucifixion. There must be an idea, thought, dream, or vision that is set before our minds to facilitate momentum. It is a redemptive privilege to see the unseen and to know the unknowable. The Holy Spirit reminds us of history and enables us to discern the future. While the present environment of ideas, moments, and people may be a reality, there is the privilege to visit tomorrow while it is today.

Law of Time

Time is past, present, and future. It has dimensions that are described by such descriptors as "temporary," "permanent," "immediate," "fullness," "soon," "later," "continuity," "discontinuity," "timely," and "timeless." Each of these descriptors must be identified and properly applied. For example, it is necessary to know the duration of events and circumstances whether they be permanent or temporary or timely or timeless. Momentum can be hindered when negative events are believed to be permanent when they are only temporary. Some things do not change with time but most things do.

Law of Perspective

We must ascribe proper value and importance to events, circumstances and even people. Momentum is enhanced when proper value is attached to the issues of life. Perspective is the recognition of the order of importance, cause, and effect. Perspective speaks of priority, and we should always put things in proper perspective, as some are heavenly or earthly and greater or lesser. Failure to do so is to make lesser issues to be greater ones. Momentum is given direction when priorities are correct.

Law of Practicality

Momentum demands our participation and rational thinking. To move by faith is not to deny the existence of the issues of life. Passivity occurs when the mind is not engaged. It is necessary to ask, look, listen, walk, and think. After all, faith is not a denial of reality but the recognition of finality. Faith takes into account the facts of life while anticipating Divine help in the process. Common sense is an indispensable attribute.

Summary

*Human existence is a cycle of growth through experiences.

*Christianity is a progressive and growing faith, which is reflected in our spiritual intelligence.

*Challenges in life provide opportunities for growth or stagnation.

*Stagnation, regression, and resistance to change are recorded in the Bible.

*Longevity and popularity are not always criteria for truth

*Longstanding of patterns of thought and behavior have emotional components.

*There is a tendency to depreciate the current beliefs and values in order to validate new ideas and thoughts.

*The desire for clarity can often be misunderstood as a resistance to change.

*Convictions must be evaluated for their accuracy and fruitfulness.

*Momentum can be hindered when we violate the laws of self-control, conviction, memory, imagination, perspective, time, and practicality.

18

IMPROVING SPIRITUAL INTELLIGENCE AND LIFE

While life offers benefits, privileges, choices, and a host of responsibilities, there is a redemptive knowledge that enables us to overcome the potential pitfalls that lurk behind every poor decision we make. While the choice of parents, race, gender, physical features, time, and geographic location of our birth are beyond our control, we do have many other choices. The choice of our mate, home, career, and friends are among the many options we can select. The outcome of these choices can be significantly improved when we engage in certain patterns of thought and behavior. The factors that improve our spiritual intelligence and, as a result, our life choices, include *repentance, transcendence, self-discipline, rehabilitation, otherliness, discernment, love, spirituality, sensitivity, accommodation, and landmarking.*

Repentance means to turn, change or accept responsibility due to wrongdoing. True repentance generates a new perspective, looking at a situation from God's point of view. It may involve the inclusion and exclusion of ideas, beliefs and even people. While repentance is classically associated with a commitment to personal change, it can represent the stabilization of thoughts and beliefs about oneself, others, and the world.

Transcendence is an awakened awareness of the dimensions of time. Nostalgia is living in the past. Fantasy is a preoccupation with dreams and the future. Of course, "contemporization" is a limited consciousness of the present world and all of its moments, events, and people. Transcendence, however, is the interconnection of the past, present, and future. It is an awareness that is indiscriminate of time, allowing new beginnings and endings based on one's purpose.

Self-Discipline is self-control of one's thoughts, attitude, and behavior. It involves self-awareness and accountability. It gives substance to dreams, for without it, they lack the behavior necessary for their fulfillment. It is not always possible to correct by verbal confession what has been created by behavior. Discipline creates integrity since it maintains the relationship between charisma and character. While skills and abilities may open many doors, it is only integrity that will keep them open. Discipline makes that possible.

Rehabilitation is the recovery and restoration of self. While it is often facilitated by the help of others, it can be a personal responsibility. It demands repentance and self-discipline to change patterns of thought and behavior. Adopting new beliefs or outlooks is the catalyst for different behavior. Similarly, our perception of our world and ourselves determine the pattern of our response. That is, when we determine our personal liabilities, responsibilities and possibilities, then self-rehabilitation is possible.

Otherliness is the awareness and concern for others. It involves the removal of self-imposed restraints placed upon human love. Selfishness is the introversion of life while otherliness is the extroversion of life. It is the willingness to accommodate different ideas, thoughts, and values without compromising personal standards of behavior. Otherliness is not self-depreciation but it is the recognition of a greater love expressed in compassion, kindness, patience, and fairness that transforms both your life and others'.

Discernment is the ability to know how, what, when, and why. It involves the identification of times, seasons, people, opportunities, privileges, and responsibilities. It enables you to hear the sound of words and listen for their meaning. It is indispensable for a productive life since it reveals proper value and meaning of all experiences. It is a product of personal encounters in the natural world of people, words, ideas, and thoughts and the spiritual world of dreams, visions, intuition, and revelation.

Love is the emulation of Jesus. It is not simply an emotion, but rather the expression of justice, benevolence, forgiveness, tolerance, and sacrifice. It is also expressed as an intolerance to injustice, an impatience with exploitation, a protest against prejudice, and an insistence to overcome poverty, ignorance, and depravity.

Spirituality is the preoccupation with God, but carnality is the preoccupation with self. Spirituality is obedience to Divine principles and practices. It is the subjection of human emotions, attitudes, and behaviors to principles and not to the force of the moment. It is the subjection of anger, greed, prejudice, pride, selfishness, and resentment to higher, more productive sentiments and actions. It is not reaction but response since the human will is not provoked nor controlled by the external environment.

Accommodation is involvement without compromise. It is the willingness to experience or entertain that which is not desired, expected, or even deserved without the loss of integrity. It is the willingness to enlarge one's personal world by including new and difference people, ideas, thoughts, and even knowledge. It involves the desire to forgive, forget, and at times to remember. Accommodation represents the ability to be involved without being entangled, or being in the world but not being of the world. Likewise, it is knowing that association does not mean identification and therefore keeping company with those of different ideas and thoughts does not mean agreement. It provides a commitment to a challenge with the understanding that there is always a beginning and an ending to everything.

Landmarking is the recognition of historic moments by remembering and recording them. It involves the recording of times of revelation, insight, healing, deliverance, provision, and understanding the things of God. David would recall how the Lord enabled him to overcome a bear, a lion, and Goliath the giant. John recorded and remembered what he saw, heard, and handled. Peter remembered when he was with Him on the holy mount and heard a heavenly voice. A landmark is something that should be honored and remembered (Prov. 22:28), so too landmarking memorializes times, moments and events that will inspire, encourage and motivate us.

The acknowledgement, adoption and manifestation of these factors yield peace and harmony with oneself and the world. They yield the momentum and character needed to accomplish goals in the natural and compliance with the spiritual. Finally, they yield, most importantly, greater spiritual intelligence.

Summary

*Greater spiritual intelligence yields better decision-making.
*Our ability to make better choices is predicated on certain patterns of thought.
*Repentance, transcendence, self-discipline, rehabilitation, otherliness, discernment, love, spirituality, sensitivity, accommodation, and landmarking influence one's attitude and behavior and yield greater spiritual intelligence.

REFERENCES

Beardsley, L., & Spry, T. (1975). *The Fulfilled Woman*. Irvine, Calif.: Harvest House Publishers.

Clouse, B., Clouse, R. G., & Culver, R. D. (1989). *Women in Ministry: Four Views*. Downers Grove, Ill.: InterVarsity Press.

Hamon, Bill. (2010). *70 Reasons For Speaking In Tongues*. Stafford, Va.: Parson Publishing House.

Handford, E. R. (1972). *Me? Obey Him?: The Obedient Wife, and God's Way of Happiness and Blessing in the Home*. Murfreesboro, Tenn.: Sword of the Lord Publishers.

Heggen, C. H. (1989). *Dominance/submission Role Beliefs, Self-Esteem and Self-Acceptance in Christian Laywomen*. New Mexico: University of New Mexico.

Helfer, R. E., & Kempe, C. H. (1974). *The Battered Child* (2d ed.). Chicago: University of Chicago Press.

Kroeger, C. C., & Beck, J. R. (1996). *Women, Abuse, and the Bible: How Scripture Can Be Used to Hurt or to Heal*. Grand Rapids, Mich.: Baker Books.

Marcovich, M. (2002). *Clementis Alexandrini Paedagogus*. Leiden u.a.: Brill.

Migne, J. (1987). *Patrologia Graeca*. Athenai: Kentron Paterikon Ekdoseon (KE. P.E.).

Miller, J. B. (1986). *Toward a New Psychology of Women* (2nd ed.). Boston: Beacon Press.

Quain, E. A. (1959). Vol. 40. *The Fathers of the Church* (p. 117). New York: Tertullian, Apologetical Works.

Seligman, M. E. (1991). *Learned Optimism: How to Change Your Mind and Your Life.* New York: A.A. Knopf.

Swidler, L. J. (1979). *Biblical Affirmations of Women.* Philadelphia: The Westminster press.

Walker, L. E. (1984). *The Battered Woman Syndrome.* New York: Springer Pub. Co.

Recommended Readings

D.R. McConnell, *A Different Gospel: A Historical and Biblical Analysis of the Modern Faith Movement*. Peabody, Mass.: Hendrickson, 1988.

S. David Moore, *The Shepherding Movement: Controversy and Christian Ecclesiology*. New York, T&T Clark International, 2003.

Michael S.B. Reid, *Strategic Level Spiritual Warfare: A Modern Mythodology: A Detailed Evaluation of the Biblical, Theological, and Historical Bases of Spiritual Warfare in Contemporary Thought*. Fairfax, Va., Xulon Press, 2002.

Joe McIntyre, E.W. *Kenyon and His Message of Faith*. Orlando, Fla., Creation House, 1997.

John F. MacArthur, Jr. *Charismatic Chaos*. Grand Rapids, Mich., Zondervan Publishing House, 1992.

CPSIA information can be obtained at www.ICGtesting.com
Printed in the USA
LVOW012015190912

299549LV00001B/3/P